THE YEAR
OF THREE POPES

Born near Manchester in 1930, Peter Hebblethwaite set out on the long course of Jesuit training at the age of seventeen. He delved into philosophy in France, picked up a first in medieval and modern languages at Oxford, and studied theology at Heythrop College when it was still in a rural setting. In 1965 he became assistant editor and shortly afterwards editor of the Jesuit periodical *The Month*. From this vantage-point he reported the final session of the Vatican Council, subsequent Roman synods, and the other major ecclesiastical events of the decade as well as the tentative beginnings of Christian-Marxist dialogue. In January 1974 he resigned from the Jesuits, while maintaining good relations with them, and began to work as a free-lance writer. His best-known articles were published in *The Observer* and devoted to the Roman Curia and the Vatican's *Ostpolitik*. Now married and living in Oxford, he writes regularly for magazines in America, Germany, Holland and France. His previous books include *Georges Bernanos*, *The Council Fathers and Atheism*, *Theology of the Church* and *The Runaway Church*.

THE YEAR
OF THREE POPES

*

Peter Hebblethwaite

COLLINS
Fount Paperbacks

First published in Fount Paperbacks
and by William Collins, London, Glasgow,
Cleveland, New York, Toronto, Sydney,
Auckland, Johannesburg, 1978

© Peter Hebblethwaite, 1978

Made and printed in Great Britain by
William Collins Sons & Co Ltd, Glasgow

Contents

Foreword

Pope Paul VI died on the evening of 6 August and two days later I was whisked to Rome by Air Mauritius, losing my luggage on the way. His successor, Pope John Paul I, died, it is assumed, late on 28 September, and I was off to Rome again. On that very day I had just completed the first version of this book which bore the title *God's Candidate* and which took the story from Pope Paul to Pope John Paul. I have decided not to omit the chapters on Pope John Paul I: they can stand as a tribute to the memory of a pontificate that was bright with hope and promise.

So instead of the story of one conclave, I found myself writing the story of two. The fascination of a conclave is obvious: it has all the excitement of a cliff-hanging contest, it is a spiritual event of great importance for the world's seven hundred million Catholics, it has drama and intrigue, it has – when you come to know them – an international cast of characters and a gallery of hangers-on who are colourful and sometimes bizarre, it has an unrivalled baroque setting, and its origins plunge deep into the Middle Ages and even touch Byzantium.

Yet the two conclaves of 1978 were also very contemporary events, reflecting the pressures, anxieties and some of the dreams of the late twentieth century. The Church and the world do not stand still. Although an out-moded apologetic attitude would have us believe otherwise, the papacy has changed and is changing, and each of the three popes discussed here has made or will make a contribution to these changes.

Thus in writing a piece of contemporary history I found myself at the same time thinking about the papacy, and soon realized that this uniquely Catholic institution had also an ecumenical interest and ecumenical implications. The ripples widen out still more when we realize that the papacy has an inescapable political dimension. It touches everyone. Though the book was swiftly written, it exploits a much longer period of reflection on the issues that arise where Church and world interact. I have often thought that we needed a new theological genre which would combine observation of what was going on with theological reflection upon it: in this way the theology springs from the event and constantly refers back to it. It becomes a meditation on one of the 'signs of the times' which Pope John XXIII, following the gospels, invited us to scrutinize.

It remains only to thank all those who by their knowledge, interpretative skills, indiscretions or simple cheerfulness made this exercise possible. I particularly need to thank Bruno Bartoloni, who readily made available his dossiers on every aspect of Italian Church life; Giancarlo Zizola, the engaging prince of Vaticanologists, from whom I learned so much; the American Jesuits Vincent O'Keefe, Don Campion, John Long and Joseph O'Hare, who made me feel at home again; Arthur Jones, editor of the *National Catholic Reporter*, Kansas City, who burst stimulatingly and generously into Rome in August; Harold Evans, editor of *The Sunday Times* in London, who sent me out to Rome twice; Hugh Kay for permission to use the substance of the article 'The Whole World His Parish' which appeared in *The Month*, September 1978; special thanks are due to Jerzy Turowicz, editor of the Krakow Catholic newspaper, who was in Rome during the October conclave, and who helped on the Polish background of Pope John Paul II; my old friend Alfred Piechowiak preserved me – I hope – from errors in the Polish language; and my colleagues at Wadham College bore patiently with my absence at an awkward time. Finally, thanks to Lady Collins who held me firmly but gently to a rash promise that I would write such a book, and cheerfully accepted all the upsets that the Holy Spirit had in store in this quite extraordinary year in the history of the papacy.

Foreword

The work is dedicated to my children, Dominic Paul and Anna Cordelia, who have seen Pope John Paul II and may reasonably expect to grow up in his reign.

Wadham College, Oxford
1 November 1978

I

The Homegoing

*When I come to die, tell them that I loved this dear world
more than I ever dared to say.*

Georges Bernanos

Giovanni Battista Montini, known to the world as Pope
Paul VI, died peacefully at 9.40 p.m. on Sunday 6 August
1978. It was the feast of the Transfiguration, an event which
reminds Christians of the Risen Christ who is present amid
the banalities of everyday existence. It was not a bad day for
him to die. Pope Paul had long anticipated his death. 'The
clock of time moves inexorably forwards,' he told pilgrims
at Castelgandolfo in 1970, 'and it points to a forthcoming
end.' In 1977, again at Castelgandolfo and on the feast of
the Assumption, he said to the assembled crowd: 'I see the
end of my life drawing near. I see myself approaching the
hereafter. It may be that we shall not celebrate this feast
together again.' Such thoughts were natural enough for a
man who was about to reach his eightieth birthday on 26
September 1977. Commentators noted the simple, direct
tone, and the avoidance of the pontifical plural. In July
1978, when he was leaving for Castelgandolfo for the last
time, he confided in Archbishop Giuseppe Caprio, the
sostituto at the Secretariat of State and his closest colla-
borator: 'We will go, but I don't know whether we will
return to Rome . . . or how we will return.'

Yet Pope Paul's death, though long anticipated, came
almost without warning. Only the day before he was still
up and about. Supper was taken as usual at 8.30 p.m. At
9.15 he recited the rosary with his two secretaries, Don

Pasquale Macchi, the Milanese patron of modern art, and Fr John Magee, an Irishman. They said compline together in the chapel. Then Pope Paul retired and had read to him a chapter of Jean Guitton's latest book (*Mon Petit Catéchisme: Dialogues avec un enfant*, Desclée de Brouwer). It was the chapter on Jesus. Guitton, who had once written a book consisting of half-remembered, half-invented dialogues with Pope Paul, had tried in his catechism to start from the questions children actually ask rather than to impose his own questions on them. A typical question is: 'Why am I Anne and why is Simone not me?' And he promised himself he would never say: 'You will find out when you are older.' That Pope Paul's last reading should have been of a work by Guitton was a reminder of his permanent debt to French culture. He was theologically formed by reading Maritain, Congar and de Lubac, and intellectually formed by Pascal, Bernanos and Simone Weil.

But despite this appearance of normality on Saturday 5 August, a fever had already developed, and its cause was diagnosed as acute cystitis. This made the arthritis from which the Pope had been suffering for a long time still more painful. He was treated with antibiotics. But he had a troubled night, and was advised to stay in bed next morning. There could be no question of appearing on the balcony for the Angelus at noon. Don Macchi agreed to say Mass for him at six o'clock. Pope Paul followed the Mass with keen attentiveness, and during the recitation of the Creed he repeated the words *apostolicam ecclesiam* twice. But by 6.15 his condition had worsened and was beginning to cause alarm. The blood pressure had increased. Breathing became more and more difficult. Messages were sent out to the Cardinal Dean (Carlo Confalonieri), the Cardinal Vicar of Rome (Ugo Poletti), the *sostituto* (Giuseppe Caprio) and the Pope's brother, Senator Ludovico Montini. He received communion under both kinds – bread and wine – and managed a friendly wave to those present. Don Macchi asked whether he would like to be anointed, and he replied '*Subito, subito*'. The Cardinal Secretary of State, Jean Villot, began the anointing, and Pope Paul clasped his hand as he prayed. He had no last messages. He continued to pray to the end. His last words were an unfinished *Our Father*. One curious detail, of which the hagiographers will make much, was that Pope Paul's alarm clock, bought long ago in the 1920s when he was on a diplomatic mission to Poland, and which had been set at 6 a.m. every day of his life, unaccountably rang at 9.40 p.m., the moment of his death.

Pope Paul's death was, in the strict sense, edifying. There was no posturing, no pretence, no forcing. And his death was not just the end of his life, but a conclusion, a gathering together in this supreme moment of what had been the meaning of his life. The thought of death tolls like a knell through modern literature, and for many it is the final proof of the absurdity of the human condition. The atheist Jean-Paul Sartre had pointed out that death cannot be rehearsed in advance – 'While we are preparing our speech from the gallows we may catch a cold and die on the way.' Pope Paul's death refuted this idea. There was a perfect match between his life and his dying: both were an expression of trust and self-giving. There was no more he could do for the 'apostolic Church' he had served.

For the next two days the Pope's body lay in state at Castelgandolfo. There was much unseemly pushing and jostling on the staircases. Women were carried out fainting. The body was watched over by two Swiss Guards whose role, it must be confessed, is more ornamental than useful. A single massive candle burned alongside the body, which was already beginning to show signs of decomposition. Pope Paul had decreed (*Romano Pontifici Eligendo*, No. 30) that no one should be allowed to photograph him either on his deathbed or after death. (He had in mind the scandal caused by Galeazzi Lisi, Pope Pius XII's doctor, who had sold photographs of the dying pope to the press and given a macabre press conference on the cause of his death.) But these instructions were widely ignored and the flashlights popped distractingly. Everyone noted the absence of tears. Italians relish grief and are not afraid to weep in public at

3

disasters. But this was felt to be more like a homegoing than a disaster.

On Wednesday 9 August the body was transported to Rome and St Peter's, at a steady pace and with a vast number of motor-cycled out-riders. Helicopters whirred overhead. Two significant events occurred on the way to St Peter's. First, the cortège stopped at St John Lateran, the cathedral church of the diocese of Rome. There Cardinal Ugo Poletti, who looked after the diocese on behalf of Pope Paul, recited a psalm. This was a reminder that the pope is, essentially, the Bishop of Rome. All his grander titles – Primate of Italy, Patriarch of the West, Pope of the Universal Church – flow from this. In the 1960s it had been argued that the pope should no longer be elected by the exclusive club of cardinals – who have no justification in scripture – but by a body more representative of the whole Church. Cardinal Suenens, for instance, had proposed that the pope be elected by the whole body of bishops or, failing that, by a selection of bishops perhaps coming together in a specially convened Synod (cf. J. de Broucker, *Le Dossier Suenens*, Editions Universitaires, Paris, 1970). Pope Paul himself seemed sympathetic to a modified version of this suggestion when on 5 May 1973 he wondered aloud whether Oriental Patriarchs and members of the Synod Secretariat – some of whom were not cardinals – should be added to the electoral college.

But, not untypically, Pope Paul launched an idea and then did not pursue it. Instead of extending the conclave, he restricted it by excluding the over-eighties in the *motu proprio, Ingravescentem Aetatem* of 1970. And in the apostolic constitution *Romano Pontifici Eligendo* of 1 October 1975 the changes he had envisaged were rejected on the grounds that 'the election of the Roman Pontiff is by ancient tradition the competence of the Church of Rome, that is of the Sacred College of Cardinals which represents her'. The difficulty was that the idea that cardinals from all over the world 'represent the Church of Rome' could only be sustained by the legal fiction that each cardinal priest is assigned a Rome parish church. Thus Cardinal Basil Hume of Westminster is

4

'responsible' for the church of San Silvestro, and Cardinal John Cody of Chicago has the church of Santa Cecilia. There is an obvious dialectic – or even tension – between the pope as Bishop of Rome and the Pope as Universal Pastor. When it is a matter of who shall elect the pope, the apostolic constitution stresses the *Roman* aspect of the event; but at the same time it asserts that the election of a new pope 'is not something unconnected with the People of God and reserved only to the college of electors but will be in a certain sense an act of the whole church' (85).

Another detail of Pope Paul's last journey stressed the Roman nature of the event. The mayor of Rome, art historian Giulio Carlo Argan, was entrusted with the safe conduct of the body from St John Lateran to St Peter's. Papal bodies have been snatched along this route before now; and the threat of the Red Brigades made a concern for security just as necessary in 1978. But Signor Argan is a Communist. No mayor of Rome could afford to ignore the death of a pope, but his active involvement suggested that the *compromesso storico*, or alliance between Christian Democrats and Communists, was still in good repair. Sealed by the death of Aldo Moro, its principal architect and a close friend of Pope Paul, it will stagger on, despite grumblings from the left of the Communist Party which feels cheated. These 'Roman' events did not point unambiguously to the conclusion that Pope Paul's successor ought to be an Italian; but they did suggest that 'the Italian factor' could not be left out of account. The renegotiation of the Concordat with Italy was one of the unfinished pieces of business on Pope Paul's desk.

Signor Argan formally handed over the body at the white marble strip at the bottom of St Peter's Square. This is where Vatican territory, officially, begins. A baritone sang a psalm *molto con vibrato*, but his efforts were drowned by the roar of the helicopters. Pope Paul was back in St Peter's, where he lay until Saturday morning. Large crowds, twelve abreast, shuffled up the centre of the aisle, between the crush barriers, to see the body. What did they go to see? And in what spirit? Piety, curiosity, devotion, ghoulishness: it was hard to know which prevailed. Italians began spontaneously to recite the rosary as they advanced, and it sounded like a murmured and lugubrious lament. Japanese tourists prepared their cameras and went snap-snap in unison. Vatican gendarmes hustled everyone past the right-hand side of the body with cries of '*Avanti, avanti*'. This last sight of Pope Paul's mortal remains was disconcerting. The face was already brown, the ear almost black: the mouth gaped open. On the other side of the body, out of sight of the crowds, two fans revolved in a vain attempt to keep the air fresh. At the Pope's own request, the body was not embalmed, and so it was exposed to the swift ravages of mortality. He had not wanted to cheat death.

This became even more evident on Friday 11 August when Pope Paul's will was published. It is a moving document of ten handwritten pages. On 30 June 1965 he had taken a sheet of notepaper embossed with the papal arms and written in his neat, clear handwriting: 'Some notes for my will. In the name of the Father and of the Son and of the Holy Spirit.' But it does not read like a will. It was as though Pope Paul, as he began the third year of his pontificate, was carried away by the drift of his meditation so that he produced not so much a will as a prayer of gratitude. The tone is Franciscan throughout. He wanted to die 'like a poor man' – *un povero*. All the glories of creation are celebrated as in St Francis' 'Canticle of the Sun'. The dominant mood is one of gratitude for all the gifts, of grace and nature, which he had received, and all the friendships which he had enjoyed.

The thought of death is omnipresent – it is after all a will – but there is no gloom. And far from making him undervalue the things of this world, they seem to acquire an enhanced value because they will so soon have to be abandoned: 'Now that the day draws to its close, and everything comes to an end, and I must leave this wonderful and turbulent world, I thank you, Lord.' There is no hint of the fretting, anxious Pope Paul whom the public thought it saw. Instead there is

6

a serene but not untested faith, and a deep sense that, though he may be pope, he still remains on the same level as his Christian brothers and sisters who share the same faith. The apostle Paul always remained a disciple. In his will he appears essentially as 'a man of the Church', not in the sense of someone who lives for and through the Church as institution, but as someone who lives intensely in the community of the Church. The Church for Pope Paul was first of all a spiritual communion. His death would be, he wrote, 'a last act of love for the Church'.

But his vision reached out beyond the Church – and here he echoed some of the themes of his first and most personal encyclical, *Ecclesiam Suam*. He saw in everyone a brother, to be helped if possible, perhaps to be saved, at any rate to be listened to and learned from. He moved easily and without strain from the dialogue with God in prayer to the more difficult dialogue with men who start from different premises. The echo of the world comes through in his prayer, but it is muted and muffled, caught up in the mysterious purposes of God.

The practical details were swiftly dealt with. Anything which had belonged to his family was to revert to his brother Ludovico. Everything else was left to the Holy See. Don Macchi was made his executor, and though he could distribute books or mementoes as he wished, he was ordered to destroy all personal notes and correspondence. He asked that his funeral be 'pious and simple', with no catafalque, and said that he wanted no monument over his grave. The notes added to the will on 16 September 1972 and 14 July 1973 confirmed these dispositions and added nothing new.

Thus our brother Paul had the simple funeral he had asked for – if one could abstract from the dignitaries and the crowd which half-filled St Peter's Square on Saturday 12 August. The coffin lay on the ground before the altar. An open Bible, its pages fluttering in the breeze, was the only adornment. The hundred or so cardinals wore red vestments – not a colour of mourning – and mitres that stressed their role as bishops. The Easter *Alleluia* was sung. *Vita mutatur, non tollitur*: life is transformed, not destroyed. Most of the music was plainchant, interspersed with throbbing solemnities from the pen of the Sistine Choir's musical director, Bertolucci. At the end an Armenian male voice choir sang a psalm of such haunting vigour that the plainsong seemed almost effete by comparison. The most significant reading was from the Gospel of St John (21: 15–19), a mysterious text on the future destiny of St Peter, who in old age would be led where he did not want to go.

But Cardinal Confalonieri, who presided as Dean of the College of Cardinals, disappointingly did not exploit this text which had been so familiar to Pope Paul. The Pope had asked that there should be no eulogy or panegyric but instead a homily: if words mean anything he was asking for a commentary on the Gospel and not a recital of his achievements. But perhaps at 85 Cardinal Confalonieri could be forgiven for not noticing the difference. He relapsed into the old style when he spoke of 'cardinals, the people of God and diplomats' – as though cardinals were not to be included in the people of God. He praised Pope Paul for his 'Credo of the People of God', a conservative document which was not the most inspiring of his pontificate.

St Peter's Square had been in grateful shadow throughout the Mass. As it came to an end towards eight o'clock – it took time to distribute Communion to the vast crowd – the moon was up over the Gianiculum Hill where a line of cypress trees was etched against the sky. Ripples of applause ran through the crowd as the body was carried into St Peter's. Handkerchiefs fluttered. Some of the distinguished guests joined in, but most did not, being unused to Roman ways. The body was buried privately in the crypt, beneath a statue of Our Lady attributed to Donatello.

So Pope Paul VI, who had wanted to be known as 'the pilgrim Pope', finally came to rest in the crypt of St Peter's, not far from Pope John XXIII whose work he had continued with such painstaking conscientiousness. And both of them lie not so very far away from the bones of St Peter, which careful scholars believe to be genuine. I could not get out of my head the Gospel of St John that had just been read. Pope Paul had used it on the day before his coronation Mass when he went to the church of San Carlo alla Corso to say farewell to his Brescia compatriots. The theme of his sermon was, 'What will become of me?' (*Che cosa sarà di me?*) His answer was that he did not know, but that, like Peter, he would be led: 'When you were young, you girded yourself and walked where you would; but when you are old, you will stretch out your hands, and another will gird you and carry you where you do not wish to go' (John 21 : 18). Where had Pope Paul been led in his long pontificate of fifteen years? And where had he led the Church?

2

Pope Paul's Heritage
to the Church

Pope Paul was timid by temperament: he became courageous out of virtue.
Jean Guitton in *Le Figaro*, 28 August 1978

The release of details about the Pope's death and the rapid publication of his will also brought out the most important change which he had introduced into the understanding of the papacy: he wanted it to be accessible. Though his sense of the Petrine mission – what he sometimes called 'the charism of Peter' – was strong and unwavering, he may be said to have 'demystified' the papacy in the sense of allowing himself to be seen as a human being. 'A Day in the Life of the Pope' became an established journalistic form (cf. Curtis Bill Pepper in the *New York Times Magazine*, 10 April 1977). Pope Pius XII had been an autocratic monarch whose aloof and mysterious private life was presented to the world as though it were 'angelic'. When Graham Greene rashly wrote an article in *The Month* in which he mentioned the famous canaries ('They walk over the table pecking at his butter, and his favourite takes crumbs from between his fingers and perches on the white shoulder', *The Month*, December 1951, p. 337), the Editor was reprimanded by the General of the Jesuits for trivializing the papacy. Pope Paul was always anxious to explain that his predecessor was not 'a heartless solitary' but a man 'of exquisite sensibility and the most delicate human sympathies'. He said this in a letter to *The Tablet* (29 June 1963) in which he defended Pope Pius against the charges made in Rolf Hochhuth's play, *The*

Representative. He argued that Pius had measured his protests in order to avoid worse reprisals.

But loyal as he was to Pius, he reacted against him in two ways: first he made sure that he could never be accused of 'not speaking out' – hence his pronouncements on every conceivable issue from 'genocide' in Biafra to the bombing of civilians in North Vietnam; and secondly he would try to be not merely a remote figure in white on a distant balcony but someone who shared, as far as he could, in the rough and tumble of ordinary life. He was available. He actually submitted to interviews with journalists, was known to eat with his secretaries, watch televison news at 8.30 p.m. and give other signs of belonging to the human race.

The iconography of successive popes gave a clue to the process that had been going on. Pius XII was almost invariably photographed alone, with arms outstretched and eyes uplifted, as though communing with the world invisible. Pope John XXIII was most often photographed with a hand raised in blessing. The typical Pauline photograph showed him sitting in an aeroplane or among a crowd of people: even when photographed kneeling in prayer – another common icon – he seemed to be humbly leading other Christians in prayer rather than enjoying some incommunicable mystical experience. The *Annuario Pontificio*, the official handbook of the Vatican, reflected the change. The Pope was no longer said to be 'now gloriously reigning'. Instead, he was described in terms of his function: 'Servant of the servants of God.' The idea of 'papacy' is not a fixed and monolithic reality which admits of no change. Nor are popes interchangeable. Each of them brings his own personality to the office and adds his own brush-strokes to the portrait. Pope Paul followed Pope John in revealing the human side of the papacy. To paraphrase Pascal, one expected to meet a pope and one met a brother.

This may not have been evident to the public at large, who saw him only from a distance. But there are many stories which show that in private he could shed the role that in public seemed so burdensome to him. Though not so folksy as the anecdotes, many of them apocryphal, which clustered round Pope John, they show that he could relax and smile. On one occasion, Fr John Magee, his English-language secretary, produced a bunch of keys to open a door in the papal apartments. Pope Paul remarked thoughtfully: 'So you have the keys – they never gave them to me.' In the late 1960s Fr Bruno Ribes S.J., at that time Editor of *Etudes*, was received in a private audience. *Etudes* had been denounced for its alleged unorthodoxy. Pope Paul remained at his desk and read out a prepared little homily on the duties of a Jesuit editor, which came down to the principle that he must defend the Church's teaching in all circumstances. The homily over, Ribes ventured to ask whether the Pope knew the source of the denunciations and whether he realized the venom and mud-slinging inaccuracy of so many right-wing publications. The conversation ran over the allotted time. Pope Paul asked for a report on the right-wing organizations. Finally he said: 'I read you a lecture when you came in here, but now I suggest that your task is much simpler: love the Church, love the Church, and then do what you will.' This pattern recurred often. In audiences with the French and Dutch bishops, he would read a prepared text and then, his sense of duty fulfilled, begin the real conversation. This 'over-flowing of the role' had been a matter of principle with Pope John. Whether he was talking with Jews or prisoners in the Ara Coeli prison or socialists in Venice, he liked to quote the text of Exodus where Joseph reveals himself to his cowed and astonished brothers: 'I am your brother Joseph.' Pope Paul had the same idea, but was less successful in communicating it to a wider public. He seemed increasingly imprisoned in his role and unable to escape from a burden which he felt as a crucifixion. 'Now I understand St Peter,' he told a Vatican diplomat in January 1973, 'he came to Rome twice, the second time to be crucified.'

A story recounted by Giancarlo Zizola illustrates another way in which Pope Paul was tragically hemmed in: by protocol (*Quale Papa?* Borla, Rome, 1977, pp. 37–39). In

November 1970 his plane landed by night at Dacca, which was still part of Pakistan at that time. A crowd of poor people had gathered on the terrace of the airport. Some of them had walked for days to get a chance to see the Pope. They included survivors of one of the greatest tragedies of the century: the floods that had swept through what was to become Bangladesh and in which over a million people perished. They waved and cheered to attract the Pope's attention. In vain. Meanwhile in the V.I.P. lounge Pope Paul was handing over a bundle of dollars to the President of Pakistan. Raimondo Manzini, Editor of *Osservatore Romano*, went over to the crowd and tried to explain why it was difficult for the Pope to meet them. There was much agitated whispering as Pope Paul finished reading his speech. Don Macchi said something to him. He came down from the dais and began to walk along the red carpet, troops either side, photographers backing away before him. Then, acting on impulse, the Pope took a few paces towards the crowd but found the way blocked by the soldiers. He tried to bless them above the heads of the troops, but he was too far away to be seen. He turned sadly back, climbed the steps into the plane, and waved farewell to Dacca. It was like an ironical commentary on what he had written in *Populorum Progressio* three years earlier: 'We were able to see and virtually to touch the very grave difficulties besetting the peoples of long-standing civilizations who are at grips with the problem of development.' How hard he had tried.

*

However, the starting-point of the conclave was not the personal psychology of Pope Paul but rather the heritage which he had left to the Church. The obituaries betrayed a certain hesitation in assessing the pontificate. Some made it easy for themselves by settling for a long and detailed chronicle of documents published, journeys made, visits received; and certainly one could only be impressed by the enormous work-load, the diversity of the problems Pope Paul had faced, the number of dossiers he had personally examined. Even allowing for the role of his collaborators, organized from 1967 onwards by the energetic Mgr (later Cardinal) Benelli, a glutton for work, the record was astonishing. But no one congratulates a pope on working hard. That goes with the job which, in human terms, has become almost impossible. It is as though the same man were expected to be Secretary General of the United Nations, President of the United States *and* Mayor of New York.

The difficulty in assessing the pontificate was particularly acute for the secular press which felt obliged to decide whether Pope Paul had been 'conservative' or 'progressive'. One favourite method, particularly in the English-speaking world, was to take a few rapid criteria of 'modernization', show that the Pope had failed to correspond to them, and thus conclude that he was a 'conservative'. If one took, for example, artificial birth-control, the ordination of married men, and the ordination of women, it was easy to show that Pope Paul had rejected all three, and tempting therefore to conclude that he had 'turned his back on the modern world'. But this was always a superficial way of judging the pontificate. An aspect of the 'Petrine office' is 'conservative' in the sense that it must hold on to the faith that has been handed down. This does not mean that Pope Paul saw tradition as the dead hand of the past weighing down on the present. True, he did have a keen sense of precedent, and a feeling that he could not in conscience give way on any of these issues without engaging the whole future of the Church. Any mistake he made would have been irrevocable. But he had a positive concept of tradition as a living reality, and believed that the full 'consent of the Church' was not yet given on any of the controverted issues. That many theologians and Catholics generally should differ from him was part of the data of the problem, but could not finally resolve it. Even today the theology of how change comes about in the Church is still rudimentary.

But it is perfectly possible to take a different starting-point and to show that Pope Paul was an innovator, and even a revolutionary in a profound sense. He chose the name of Paul deliberately. In Roman rhetoric Peter is the figure of stability and order, while Paul represents the adventurous, outgoing, missionary element. At least in the first phase of his pontificate, Pope Paul was resolutely Pauline.

When he became Pope in 1963, the Second Vatican Council had finished one rather inconclusive session: the battle-grounds of the future had been staked out. It is notoriously easier to begin a Council than to conclude one, and Pope Paul guided it through three more sessions with great skill, avoiding the open revolt that was always threatening from the hard-core of conservatives (among whom was a certain Archbishop Marcel Lefebvre), and securing in the end a large measure of consensus. He said that his aim was that there should be '*pas de vaincus, mais de convaincus*' – that no one should feel he had been defeated, and that all should be personally convinced of what the Council had done. Thereafter the implementation of the Council was the key to his entire policy. He glimpsed, too, that the changed self-understanding of the Church involved a changed self-understanding of the papal ministry. If all ministry was for service, then so was the papal ministry. The papacy became less of a power and more of a service to the whole Church. Pope John had said that 'the Church is for all, but especially for the poor'; Pope Paul sold his tiara and gave the money away to the poor. There could be no clearer sign that something had changed.

He pressed ahead with liturgical change, despite opposition that was bitter and, eventually, schismatic. The liturgical debate became confused because those who resented the loss of the old turned it so often into a debate about aesthetics, and it was easy to contrast the august 'sense of mystery' of the Tridentine rite (at its best) with the supermarket English and the limp guitar chords of the new rite (at its worst). But the aim of liturgical change was pastoral rather than aesthetic. It was based on the simple principle that liturgy should communicate, and one could not communicate in a language that few people really knew. A Jesuit was once asked by a group of nuns to say Mass in Latin: he agreed, provided they would also accept a homily in Latin, which they sat through in stolidly uncomprehending silence. The Council's understanding of the Eucharist placed it at the centre of Christian life. In the Acts of the Apostles we read of how the first Christians 'devoted themselves to the apostles' teaching and fellowship, to the breaking of bread and the prayers' (Acts 2 : 42). There one could discern in essential outline the pattern of the Mass: the Gospel is proclaimed in the liturgy of the Word, and then communion in the breaking of bread forges the unity of the Church and sets it off on its mission in the world. These simple principles had consequences over the whole range of theological thinking (they have been explained in *The Runaway Church*, chapter 2, 'They Have Robbed Us of Our Liturgy', Collins, Fount Paperbacks, 1978) : priestly ministry looks different when the priest is seen in terms 'of the community he has to serve and build up; the local church acquires greater importance as the place where Christians actually are.

Pope Paul's commitment to the pastoral changes in the liturgy was never in doubt. It cost him a lot. There was no doubt that 'excesses' and rather wild improvisations were taking place in some parts of the world, and he periodically denounced them in somewhat vague terms. But he always balanced this by denouncing equally those who resisted all change. In the second half of the pontificate the relative success gained by Archbishop Marcel Lefebvre showed that nostalgia was alive and well and living at Ecône in Switzerland. Some thought that Pope Paul made a tactical mistake in dealing with the Lefebvre affair. After a commission of cardinals had given a negative report on Ecône and it had no effect, Pope Paul engaged his own personal responsibility and arranged a meeting with the recalcitrant Archbishop. He quite reasonably felt that in a personal meeting with someone who held (or so he kept saying) an exalted view of the papal office, he would be able to appeal to Lefebvre's conscience and persuade him to give up his systematic opposition to the Council. The meeting took place and, like everything else, it failed. Pope Paul was snubbed and rebuffed. He had tried the ultimate deterrent and it had not worked. There was nothing more he could do: excommunication, though it was talked about in the summer of 1977 when Lefebvre ordained a number of priests at Ecône, was not his style. So he buried the whole affair in another commission of cardinals who were given the ungrateful task of reading the entire works of Lefebvre. As far as is known, they are still busily reading.

Among the liturgical reforms was a revival of the rite of concelebration. When the priests of a diocese gathered round their bishop to celebrate the Eucharist with him, or when the bishops of the world gathered round the pope, there was a vivid and tangible expression of 'collegiality'. In plain terms this meant that all the world's bishops shared with the pope responsibility for the whole Church. Collegiality dealt a blow to the idea of a separated, aloof and monarchical papacy which would be set over against the rest of the Church. But collegiality, if it were not merely to remain on the drawing-board, needed some practical instrument by which it could be expressed. In response to requests made at the Council, Pope Paul set up the Synod of Bishops in a *motu proprio* dated 15 September 1965. Its function was 'to inform and give advice' to the pope, and it was said that in certain circumstances it might be granted 'deliberative power', i.e. the right to decide certain questions. It was hoped by many that the Synod would act as a counter-weight to the Roman Curia, which always had a tendency to act independently, and there were spasmodic attempts to make the Synod a place where the heads of Roman Congregations could be cross-questioned as in a parliament. These attempts failed because 'open government' was such a novelty in the Church, but it was good that the principle of accountability should have at least been stated.

There have been in all five Synods. In 1967 there were five topics: the revision of canon law, doctrine, seminaries, mixed marriages and liturgy. In 1969 there was a special or 'extraordinary' Synod to deal with the problem of 'collegiality' in the aftermath of *Humanae Vitae*. 1971 was devoted to the priestly ministry and justice in the world. It was probably the Synod's finest hour so far and did much to make the work of the Pontifical Justice and Peace Commission known to Catholics generally. 1974 studied the theme of evangelization, reached an impasse, handed a list of unresolved questions to the Pope, and indirectly contributed to his apostolic exhortation *Evangelii Nuntiandi* of 8 December 1975. This important document is a heart-felt plea for unity within the Church, without which the work of evangelization will not get off the ground. Pope Paul wrote:

> The power of evangelization will find itself considerably reduced if those who proclaim the Gospel are divided among themselves in all sorts of ways. Is this not perhaps one of the great sicknesses of evangelization today? Indeed, if the Gospel which we proclaim is seen to be rent by doctrinal disputes, ideological polarizations or mutual condemnations among Christians . . . how can those to whom we address our preaching fail to be disturbed, disorientated or even scandalized? (No. 77).

The last Synod of the pontificate took place in 1977 and it tackled catechetical problems. Those who have taken part in the various Synods have usually come out smiling gamely. Observers have noted a gradual emasculation of the institution. It has not really been trusted enough to be effective. Still, the Synod is there, is unlikely to be abolished, and forms an important part of the inheritance.

Oddly enough, it was the two questions which Pope Paul refused to submit to the collegial process that caused him the most trouble. Once again he engaged his personal authority where he might have sheltered behind his fellow bishops. Birth-control and clerical celibacy were first withdrawn from the competence of the Council, and then 'dealt with' in successive encyclical letters, *Sacerdotalis Coelibatus* of 1967 and *Humanae Vitae* of 1968. It is difficult to know exactly why Pope Paul could not trust his fellow bishops on these two issues: was it a matter of conscience for him, that he could not shuffle off onto others, or did he have a private feeling that the world's bishops would come up with an answer that he considered mistaken? The two questions, of course, were different in nature and had a different theological status. Clerical celibacy might be, as he wrote in the opening sentence of *Sacerdotalis Coelibatus*, 'a most precious jewel in the crown of the Church', but no one could claim that it was of the essence of the priesthood since his predecessor St Peter and many priests of Oriental Churches in communion with Rome had undoubtedly been married. Though many 'congruent' reasons could be advanced for celibacy – availability, total dedication and so on – none of them were absolutely decisive and most of them applied more directly to monastic or religious life. Clerical celibacy, therefore, remained a matter of discipline rather than of doctrine.

Humanae Vitae touched more people more directly. It affected an area in which an elderly celibate might not be thought to be wholly competent. It made a different claim: it said that the natural law, which the Church has the right to interpret, rejected the whole notion of artificial birth-control while accepting the hazardous rhythm method. And it came after the majority of a specially set up commission had reached precisely the opposite conclusion. With *Humanae Vitae* Pope Paul had made the fateful mistake of consulting experts and bishops and then ignoring those whom he had consulted. And the paradox of the whole affair was that the attempt to reassert separated papal authority resulted in the weakening of it. For both the questions he reserved to himself involved issues of personal liberty about which the late twentieth century is extremely sensitive. The upshot was that documents intended to 'settle' a question once and for all stimulated discussion and made it more lively; and it was not only opposition to birth-control and clerical celibacy that came under attack, but papal authority itself. Pope Paul's sense of being misunderstood grew. It was another thorn in his crown of thorns.

If Pope Paul's attitude to collegiality, after a burst of early enthusiasm, remained cool, the same cannot be said of his attitude to ecumenism. Here he showed none of that hesitation, that *amletismo*, which was so often said to characterize him. Once more, we can see how revolutionary he was if we set his work in historical perspective. In 1928 Pope Pius XI poured ill-disguised scorn on the nascent ecumenical movement. 'Congresses and meetings are arranged,' he wrote in *Mortalium Animos*, 'attended by a large concourse of hearers, where all without distinction, unbelievers as well as every kind of Christian, even those who have unhappily rejected Christ and denied his divine nature and mission, are invited to join in the discussion.' Ecumenism, in fact, was a short cut to 'indifferentism', the idea that it did not really matter what you believed. Pope Paul, on the other hand, began from the conciliar perception that ecumenism was the work of the Holy Spirit, which is the Christian way of declaring that it is a Good Thing. He once said that 'ecumenism is the most mysterious part of our Petrine mission', but that did not lead him to abandon it.

For 'mysterious' we should perhaps read 'mystical'. By that I mean nothing esoteric, but simply the sense of being 'led by the Spirit' down unfamiliar paths. The way was not altogether clear, it was shrouded by mists, but the vision of the final goal was obscurely glimpsed: union in Christ through the power of the Holy Spirit who is Love. During the final session of the Council there was an ecumenical service at St Paul Without the Walls. Pope Paul told a strange and moving story which came from Soloviev, the great Russian Orthodox theologian. A visitor had gone to stay in a monastery to discuss his spiritual problems. After talking with one of the monks until late at night, he could not find his way through the darkened passages to the room assigned to him. So he slept in the corridor. Next morning he woke up to find that he had been sleeping outside his own room. . . . Pope Paul left his hearers to draw their own conclusion from this parable.

Much of Pope Paul's ecumenism took the form not of doctrinal statements but of lived parables or 'gestures'. But it is important to realize that the 'gestures' were neither

gimmicky nor empty. The Orthodox have a better understanding of this point than Western Christians who are less
able to read sacramental language. Thus for the Orthodox
theologian Jean Meyendorff, the fact that Pope Paul went
to Istanbul in 1967, that he embraced Patriarch Athenagoras
and sat side by side with him, reversed a thousand years
of history in which Rome had claimed universal and immediate jurisdiction. True, the gesture needed interpretation
and doctrinal clarification, but it had brought a new element
into the situation (cf. 'Rome and Orthodoxy: Authority or
Truth' in *A Pope for All Christians?*, Paulist Press, New York,
1976, and SPCK, London, 1977, p. 139). The text handed
over on that occasion tried to explain the gesture: 'Now,
after a long period of division and reciprocal misunderstanding,' it said, 'it occurs, by the grace of God, that our
Churches recognize each other as sisters once more' (*Anno
Ineunte*, 25 July 1967). But Pope Paul went further than that,
and on 15 December 1975, when receiving a mission from
the Constantinople Patriarch in the Sistine Chapel, he suddenly knelt down before Metropolitan Melitone and kissed
his feet. The astonished Metropolitan was rather flustered,
could not think what to do, tried to kneel down himself
but was restrained by Pope Paul. Patriarch Dimitrios I of
Constantinople interpreted the gesture a few days later: 'The
Pope has proved to the Church and to the whole world
that he is what he should be: a Christian bishop and above
all the first bishop of Christendom, the Bishop of Rome,
that is a reconciling and unifying bridge between the Church
and the world.'

Anglicans, too, were treated to a number of spectacular
gestures. When Archbishop Fisher had visited Pope John
unofficially in 1960, the whole affair, according to Peter
Nicholls, 'was treated like a guilty secret. No photograph
was permitted and every effort was made for the event to
pass as unobtrusively as possible' (*The Politics of the Vatican*,
Praeger, New York, 1968, p. 314). When his successor,
Dr Michael Ramsey, visited the Vatican in 1966, he was
received in the Sistine Chapel and embraced as a brother

Patriarch. Pope Paul explained: 'By your coming you rebuild a bridge which for centuries has lain fallen between the Church of Rome and Canterbury.' The polemical past was consigned to 'the hands of the God of mercy'. The next decade saw intense bridge-building activity as the Anglican/Roman Catholic International Theological Commission hammered out its three agreed statements on the Eucharist, Ministry and Authority. It is not wholly irrelevant that two of their meetings were held in Venice where the Patriarch, Albino Luciani, supplied the theologians with ice-cream and bottles of wine. Even the canonization of the English and Welsh Martyrs in 1970, which at first looked as though it would jeopardize good relations between the two Churches, was turned to good account by Pope Paul. He said:

> May the blood of these martyrs be able to heal the great wound inflicted on God's Church by reason of the separation of the Anglican Church from the Catholic Church. . . . Their devotion to their country gives us the assurance that on the day when – God willing – the unity of faith and life is restored, no offence will be inflicted on the honour and sovereignty of a great country such as England. There will be no seeking to lessen the legitimate prestige and usage proper to the Anglican Church when the Roman Catholic Church – this humble 'servant of the servants of God' – is able to embrace firmly her ever-beloved sister in the one authentic communion of the family of Christ: a communion of origin and faith, a communion of priesthood and rule, a communion of the saints in the freedom and love of the spirit of Jesus.

Perhaps the most important feature of this passage was that Pope Paul wrote it himself and added it to his address at the last moment. His speech-writers were taken by surprise, and the Secretariat for Christian Unity was delighted.

Liturgical reform, collegiality, ecumenism: these were the three main elements of the inheritance Pope Paul left to the Church and to his successor. They were all directly inspired by the Second Vatican Council which provided him with a policy for his entire pontificate — sometimes even naïvely so. When he visited a flooded Rome suburb in the late 1960s he gravely explained to the astonished victims: 'I am here because of the Council.' They imagined he might just have come to see them. But he needed the Council to justify his departures from precedent. It must be added, however, that as the Council receded into the past, Pope Paul seemed to shrink back from the more adventurous and Pauline early years of his pontificate. The Congregation for the Doctrine of Faith (formerly known as the Holy Office) was allowed to mangle, on doctrinal grounds, the proposed new rite of penance and showed itself hostile to the idea of General Absolution. Dr Donald Coggan's welcome in Rome in April 1977 was noticeably less enthusiastic than that of his predecessor: in the mean time the Anglicans were wondering whether or not to ordain women, and Dr Coggan made a plea for inter-communion now which was regarded as tactless. He is a man who speaks his mind and does not beat about the ecumenical bush. The result was, however, that towards the end of the pontificate one member of the Secretariat for Christian Unity gloomily confided: 'It's all very well to call them sister churches, but just try treating them as sister churches and see what happens.'

Obviously, these distressing developments owed something to old age and to the growing importance of subordinates. Pope Paul himself in the 1950s had remarked on the danger of a long pontificate: the pope runs out of steam and has exhausted his imaginative capacity; routine sets in; the pontificate becomes a holding operation. Resignation was contemplated but always rejected: Pope Paul felt that universal paternity could not be resigned and that he would have to soldier on till the end. 'They treat him as though he were already dead' was the cruel comment of one Vatican official in 1975.

Here one has to mention the role of the Roman Curia. It is a mixed body of 2,260 men (and a few women) who, especially at the middle levels, are highly competent and theologically alive. The Curia is at the service of the pope, and if the pope is a centralizer, then the Curia will inevitably be centralizing; if he is a collegial pope, then the Curia too would have to learn the habit of consultation. One principle that has been regularly observed only by the Secretariat for Christian Unity is that drafts of all important documents are supposed to be sent to all the world's bishops for their comments. They should not learn about them from the newspapers. No one disputes that reform of the Roman Curia is still urgently needed. Two reports lie on the desk of the new Pope. The first was written by the late Cardinal Luigi Traglia, and is concerned with how the reforms of 1967 are actually working: it points out, among other things, that there is still a grave lack of co-ordination on certain questions. Marriage, for instance, can fall under the Congregation for the Doctrine of Faith when it is a matter of certain annulments, but the Congregation of the Sacraments also has an interest in marriage; the Secretariat for Christian Unity is concerned about 'mixed marriages' (or 'ecumenical marriages' as they are more positively called) and, just to compound the confusion, there now exists a special Committee on the Family. The second report is more recent. It is the work of Archbishop Gagnon's commission and they interviewed every member of the Roman Curia. Inspired partly by financial considerations and in the expectation that an axe might somewhere be wielded, it will give the new pope much food for thought as he sets about his pontificate.

Pope Paul left one further legacy to his successor: the apostolic constitution, *Romano Pontifici Eligendo*, which laid down the rules about how the conclave should be conducted. It is a document of uncompromising fierceness. It makes no mention of either collegiality or ecumenism: it could be said that there is no reason why it should. But as Paul Johnson remarked, it could have been written at any time during the last thousand years, except for its warning against electronic bugging devices. It imposes the most stringent conditions of secrecy on the conclave, and enshrines the full panoply of papal power. Among the many oaths which had to be sworn by the cardinals, under pain of excommunication, was this: 'We likewise promise, bind ourselves and swear that whichever of us by divine disposition is elected Roman Pontiff will not cease to affirm, defend and if necessary vindicate integrally and strenuously the spiritual and temporal rights and the liberty of the Holy See' (No. 49). That sounded very much like a pre-emptive strike against the theologians whose work is discussed in the Appendix, and who would have the papacy renounce power in order to gain authority. But there is another aspect of the inheritance of Pope Paul that deserves special treatment: his diplomatic activity, where the balance-sheet is more positive.

The inheritance to the Church discussed in this chapter remains ambivalent because of the disparity between the admirable principles Pope Paul stated on collegiality, liturgical reform and ecumenism, and his inconsistent practice. In the end, the Petrine principle of conservation came to prevail. Conservatives welcomed this, and said that Pope Paul had at last come to his senses and called a halt to the dangerous process of devolution in the Church; but others regretted that the Pauline spirit had been overlaid with paralysing caution.

3

The Whole World His Parish

> *In his work for peace, the Pope has the whole world for his parish and the whole human race for his flock.*
> Arnold Toynbee in *The Vatican and World Peace* (Edited by Francis Sweeney S.J., Colin Smythe, 1970, p. 31)

Pope Paul's inheritance to the Church has so far been considered within the life of the Church and its specifically religious mission. But the Church exists in the world, and the papacy has necessarily a political dimension. The Pope can act on the world through the visits he receives from statesmen, the journeys he makes, and the activity of his diplomatic corps. Of course it would be absurd to reduce the theological question of the relationship of Church and world to papal diplomatic activity: all Christians are willy-nilly involved in the world, and have to be inventive and to discover God's grace at work wherever they happen to be. Papal diplomatic activity does not dispense them from commitment. But it would be equally absurd to underestimate the role which the Pope plays on the international scene.

Like his two immediate predecessors, Pope Paul VI was a papal diplomat by professional training. He had thought long and hard about the purposes of Vatican diplomacy. The Pope, as Stalin knew, has no divisions at his command. Nor can he juggle with technical know-how or trade deals. These facts, together with the peculiar nature in international law of Vatican sovereignty (cf. Pio Ciprotti, 'The Holy See: Its Form, Function and Status', *Concilium*, October 1970), mean that pontifical diplomatic activity is unique. It is not concerned with the defence and promotion of national interests, and the role of the diminutive Vatican City State is to provide a way of access to the international scene. As long ago as 1951 Mgr Montini, who was at that time *sostituto* in the Secretariat of State, defined diplomacy in general as

> the art of creating and maintaining international order, that is to say peace, not by means of force or by the balancing of material interests, but by way of open and responsible settlements (*Paolo VI e la Pontificia Accademia Ecclesiastica*, 1965, p. 22).

Twenty-five years later the Holy See signed the final declaration of the Helsinki Conference on Security and Co-operation. Whatever one might think of the Helsinki Declaration – and no sooner was the ink dry than there were loud complaints that nothing had really changed – for Pope Paul it represented a step beyond the 'balance of terror' and an attempt to move towards 'an open and responsible settlement' in Post-War Europe. From this point of view, the continuity in the aims of pontifical diplomacy from Pius XII to Paul VI is striking.

In the 1951 speech Mgr Montini also spoke of the specific role of the Church in 'the world'. The aim of Vatican diplomacy was not to secure a privileged place for the Church:

> The Church of today should not base its strength and its prosperity on the support of states, but should depend upon the word and the strength which she bears in her heart, by divine institution: the Church needs liberty, not bonds.

With this speech the ghost of temporal sovereignty was finally laid to rest, and the nineteenth century may be said to have come to an end. The Holy See was clearly seen not as a 'power', seeking support from other comparable 'powers', but as the representative of a spiritual force whose authentication came from elsewhere. And as such, the Holy See asserts its freedom as much from friendly governments that would strive to 'recuperate' the Church as from hostile governments who would persecute her. Again, twenty-five years later, the renegotiation of the Concordat with Spain proved as difficult an exercise as the attempt to regularize relations with the Polish government. In both cases the goal remained the same: *Une Eglise libre dans un état libre.* The maxim came from Cavour, a secular and liberal source who was not always candidly acknowledged.

But however much one may legitimately stress the continuity of Vatican diplomatic activity, it is undeniable that when Cardinal Montini became Pope Paul VI in 1963, he had to face a radically changed situation. His predecessor, Pope John XXIII, had initiated a cautious dialogue with communist leaders on which Pope Paul was to build. There was a move 'from anathema to dialogue' in Roger Garaudy's phrase, and the cold war came to a provisional end. The other major novelty was the ending of the colonial period and the emergence of new and youthful nations, especially in Africa and the Far East. If the opening to the communist world was reflected in Pope Paul's first encyclical, *Ecclesiam Suam*, another encyclical, *Populorum Progressio*, placed the Church firmly on the side of development and what was becoming known as the 'third world'. The *Wall Street Journal* dismissed *Populorum Progressio* as 'souped-up Marxism', which showed that it was to be taken seriously. It was not difficult to infer the papal analysis of the world situation: however important the East-West conflict and its resolution might be, the future of the world would be shaped by the answer it gave to the North-South conflict. Speaking on his name-day in 1970, Pope Paul said:

> There rises from the Third World a cry for help. Trusting expectation is turning into terrible denunciation which could explode . . . and have lethal consequences for peace and true progress.

'You may, and you must, have an African Christianity,'
Pope Paul had told the African Bishops assembled at Kampala in 1969, and though he later cast doubts on the possibility of a specifically African theology, he clearly understood
the growing influence of nationalism as a legitimate, though
not absolute, aspiration.

If Pius XII could be called – he had not much choice –
'the Pope of the Atlantic Alliance' and John XXIII 'the
Pope of the opening to the East', Pope Paul VI merited the
title of 'Pope of the third world'. One could note that this
new emphasis corresponded not only to a changed world
situation in which third world countries, though still econo-
mically weak and dependent, had an important role to play
in the United Nations and its specialized agencies, but also
to an imminent change in the distribution of Catholics
throughout the world. Whereas in 1960 the Catholics of
Europe and North America made up 51% of the total
number, the projection for the year 2000 is that by then they
will be reduced to a mere 30% while the remaining 70%
will be from the third world. It is not for nothing that 'We
think in centuries here' is a favourite Roman saying.

Before discussing the event of the Council, which in one
sense challenged and in another gave fresh impetus to the
Vatican diplomatic corps, it would be useful to set down the
means by which Pope Paul sought to pursue his long-term
aims. Papal diplomacy has a strongly personal character,
partly because popes are more durable than contemporary
statesmen, and partly because of the uniqueness of the office.
State visits to the Vatican increased notably during Pope
Paul's pontificate. There were 10 to Pius XI, 26 to Pius
XII, 34 to John XXIII, and well over 90 to Pope Paul.
The eagerness with which world leaders sought to meet him
was truly astonishing. They ranged from Mrs Golda Meir
to President Tito, from Field-Marshal Idi Amin to Prime
Minister Edward Heath, from President Podgorny to Presi-
dent Nixon. Communist leaders were particularly assiduous
in their visits, and oddly anxious to get the protocol right.
Their motivations no doubt varied, and opportunism has

not always been absent, but to Rome they trooped in unprecedented numbers.

In his name-day address of 1973 Pope Paul gave his own explanation of this phenomenon. He said that 'The nations find in the Holy See a direction, a moral inspiration that all, however confusedly, feel should animate and guide the life of nations and their dealings with each other.' And the way to achieve this end, he added, was not by preaching to the nations, but 'by participating, as a member with full rights, although having particular characteristics of its own, in the life of the international community.' The importance of international organizations had been greatly enhanced during the pontificate of Pope Paul and he saw the Church's participation in their work as one way of being 'present to the world'. '*Jamais plus la guerre, jamais plus la guerre*', he had pleaded in his appeal to the United Nations in New York in 1965, and he remained true to this insight. The Church is also in an analogous sense 'an international organization', and Pope Paul saw Vatican diplomacy as a way of representing the claims of conscience and morality in a world where power politics tend to prevail. The Church could be 'the voice of those who have no voice', as the 1971 Synod put it.

Apart from his personal influence, which was greatly amplified by his journeys (until they ceased in 1970), the principal agency through which the Pope could act was the papal diplomatic corps. It was directly responsible to the Secretariat of State which, from 1967 onwards, was animated by Mgr Giovanni Benelli, the *sostituto*. The Cardinal Secretary of State, Jean Villot, busied himself rather with relationships between episcopal conferences. The number of papal envoys grew as new states came into existence. When they were all summoned to a conference at Frascati near Rome in September 1973 they numbered 36 nuncios, 36 pronuncios, 16 apostolic delegates and one chargé d'affaires. Though small by comparison with the State Department or the Foreign Office, the network of papal diplomats provided useful listening posts in most of the world's trouble spots.

Not to be neglected in any consideration of Vatican diplomacy is Vatican Radio, which by its selection of news items had a special role to play with its broadcasts to Eastern Europe and to Africa. Thus there was in theory a two-way system of communication.

The Council did not discuss at any length the papal diplomatic corps, though the decree *On Bishops* asked that 'in view of the pastoral role of bishops, the office of Legates of the Roman Pontiff be more precisely determined' (9). This comparative reticence is easily explained. Every office in the Church was scrutinized by Vatican II except the papacy itself, since, the theory ran, Vatican I had dealt with the papacy. Nevertheless, the result of the Council was that the whole system of Vatican diplomacy seemed a legacy from the past which could not easily be fitted into the new self-understanding of the Church. If collegiality were to be stressed, and with it the autonomy of the local churches, then the local bishops were the 'papal representatives' for their area and another set of representatives seemed somewhat redundant. Moreover, the dual function of papal envoys as representatives both to the state and the local bishops could be a cause of friction and awkwardness. Cardinal Suenens once referred to them as 'spies on the local churches', and certainly they exercised great influence if only because episcopal nominations passed through their hands. Some papal diplomats showed great keenness in forwarding to Rome press clippings of selected remarks of theologians held to be dangerous. There was another reason why they came under attack. The Church's 'presence to the world', as understood by the Council in *Gaudium et Spes*, could never be exhaustively expressed by initiatives emanating from the Holy See. The main thrust of the Council was to make the whole Church, and especially the laity, active in the secular world. In short the papal diplomatic corps seemed rather anomalous in the post-conciliar situation.

Pope Paul was most reluctant to abandon an institution in which he had grown up and of which he knew the proven value on the international scene. If he could not abandon it, he could at least respond to the wishes of the Council and reform it. This task was undertaken in the Apostolic Letter *Sollicitudo Omnium Ecclesiarum* dated 24 June 1969. It contained an important change of emphasis which reversed the order of priorities set down in the 1917 Code of Canon Law. It stated clearly that 'the primary and specific purpose of the mission of the Pontifical Representative is to render ever closer and more operative the ties that bind the Apostolic See and the local churches.' This was to emphasize the pastoral role of papal diplomats and their need to be sensitive to local needs. Only then was the second function stated as follows: 'Upon the Pontifical Representative also falls the duty of safeguarding, in co-operation with the Bishops, the interests of the Church and the Holy See in his relations with the civil authorities of the country where he exercises his office' (IV).

A statement of priorities could not be expected to solve all problems at a stroke. Nor did it. But it is a theme to which Pope Paul constantly returned. Addressing his envoys to the Far East gathered at Manila in 1970, he said:

> The nuncio's role is also evolving. Until now the nuncio was little more than the Pope's representative to governments and churches. Above all his activity was of an hierarchical and administrative nature; in a certain sense he remained a stranger to the local church.

There would have been no point in making this remark unless radical change was expected. Vatican diplomats responded diversely, as one might expect. In Chile they found their nunciature daubed with left-wing slogans which alleged their complicity with the rich. Elsewhere they could discreetly help a sleepy local church to implement the Council. In Spain they renewed the episcopate and so prepared change. One useful function of papal diplomats has not been brought out even by apologists. In a situation of political instability, the papal representative could act as a lightning-conductor. Or, to change the metaphor, the diplomat could act as a buffer between the local bishops and their government. If the government fell or was violently overthrown, the 'distance' of the bishops meant that they would not be dragged down in its fall. It was much easier to remove and replace a nuncio.

The paradoxical result of the inner-Church controversy on the role of papal diplomats has been that they have often been more effective in dealing with secular authorities who appreciate their role rather than with local churches who may have their doubts. This was another thorn in Pope Paul's crown of thorns. Diplomacy was his home ground, his *métier*, and he several times presented a full-scale apologia for the art of diplomacy. In 1968 he told the members of the diplomatic corps accredited to the Holy See that 'to despair of diplomacy is to despair of man'. Modern warfare had made the option clearer than ever: diplomacy is the only alternative to total destruction. He did not quite say that jaw-jaw is better than war-war, but he came close to it. And the lofty principles which for him governed Vatican diplomatic activity were stated with clarity:

> Diplomacy is the art of creating among peoples humane and reasonable relations animated by a high ideal, and aiming at establishing the rule of law, justice and peace in the international community (quoted by Archbishop Cardinale in *The Vatican and World Peace*, ed. by Francis Sweeney S.J., Colin Smythe, 1970, p. 96).

Of its nature much of the work of diplomacy is invisible. Publicly messages are exchanged, envoys are dispatched and occasionally mediation is proposed (it resolved a minor conflict in San Domingo), but the public record does not reveal the whole story. Pope Paul was convinced that the Church, through the Holy See, could make a distinctive contribution to international affairs. He tried to spell this out in his 1970 speech to the College of Cardinals:

> Strong in faith, unshakeable in hope and moved by a love

without limit, the Church goes out to meet the oldest religions as well as the most recent ideologies ... to bring to them her secret and her treasure. These are not those of a perfected organization or tested technology, but 'a seed, a leaven, salt and light', and she brings them with very simple words which everyone understands as a promise and a liberation. 'She speaks of truth, justice, liberty, progress, concord, peace, civilization' (*ibid*. The quotations are from *Ecclesiam Suam*).

The novelty of this position should not be under-estimated. Pope Paul saw the Church not as 'over against' a world that was hostile and misled, but rather as sharing with the world a common destiny and building upon its deepest aspirations. The world is not so much judged as under-pinned in its best endeavours.

This 'openness to the world' included an openness to 'the most recent ideologies'. There is no doubt that the phrase was intended to refer to Communism, and the Pope's *Ostpolitik* was one of the most striking and controversial features of his pontificate. Pope John had made the initial breakthrough by distinguishing between the error – which must be rejected – and the man who errs, who has not thereby forfeited his human rights. In 1961 he sent Mgr Casaroli to Vienna for a conference on consular rights and he was able to make contact with communist diplomats for the first time. Pope Paul confirmed Casaroli in this work and he became known, not wholly inappropriately, as 'the Henry Kissinger of the Vatican'. Mgr Casaroli has always maintained that the Church had been waiting all the time with arms outstretched, and therefore had not changed its attitude: the novelty of the situation was that the Communists had changed. In support of this view he was able to quote the nuancé remark of *Ecclesiam Suam*: 'It could be said that it is not so much that we condemn these systems and regimes as that they express their radical opposition to us in thought and deed.' If, then, their opposition proved to be less than radical, if for whatever reason they were now prepared to talk, the opportunity must be seized with eagerness but not with naïveté.

The difficulty with the *Ostpolitik* was that from the outset it had to work on two levels and had two distinct goals. It could be seen as an international matter, a contribution towards peace and *détente*, and this aspect was uppermost in the thinking of Pope Paul and Mgr Agostino Casaroli. But international *détente* was simultaneously thought of as the best framework within which the lot of Catholics living in communist regimes could be improved. The practical pastoral goal was contained within the international political goal. But to many Catholics in Eastern Europe, and still more to exiles in the West, the very act of talking to communist leaders was an insult to the martyrs of their churches, a betrayal of their sacrifice. The case of Cardinal Mindszenty summed up the dilemma facing the Vatican. He was undoubtedly a great hero of the faith who had known torture and intense anguish in communist prisons. Yet at the same time by his presence in the American Embassy in Vienna he was an obstacle to *détente* and to better relations with the Hungarian government. Eventually he succumbed to personal appeals from the Pope to leave Budapest – Cardinal König acted as intermediary – but once released he produced a bitter book of *Memoirs* and died a disappointed man, a casualty of *détente*.

But it was always a caricature   encouraged by Archbishop Lefebvre among others – to present Pope Paul and Mgr Casaroli as feeble and gullible compromisers in contrast with the intransigence of the faithful Mindszenty. Neither Pope Paul nor Casaroli were under any illusions about what they were doing. In exchange for co-operation on peace and disarmament, desirable goals in themselves, they hoped to secure more favorable conditions for the Catholics of Eastern Europe who numbered sixty million. In a way this was a return to the most traditional principles of Vatican diplomacy. Pius XI had said that he would talk with the devil if it were necessary for the good of souls. And in Eastern Europe the aim of the *Ostpolitik* was to secure first the *esse* of the Church, its right to exist at all; then one could hope to move, inch by inch, towards the *bene esse* of the Church in which she enjoys the right to nominate bishops freely and to catechize children, to build churches and have newspapers; ahead would lie the shimmering horizon of *plene esse* in which the Church would have full freedom to exercise its mission. No one would claim that this happy state has even begun to be achieved anywhere in Eastern Europe. Agreements in Hungary have proved fragile or have subjugated the Church. In Czechoslovakia there is no question of any agreements at all. But it would be difficult to deny that some progress has been made, especially in Poland where the Church is sociologically strong, and in the German Democratic Republic where it is weak. And if the only alternative usually proposed to Pope Paul's *Ostpolitik* was a return to the exchange of abuse found in the cold war period (as some angry Ukrainians have – understandably – suggested), then it is difficult to see how that would have helped the Catholics of Eastern Europe.

For completeness one has to add that China was not excluded from the papal vision. In his UNO speech in 1965 the Pope proposed the admission of China to that body. At the Epiphany in 1967 he startled the Taiwan diplomats present by suggesting that diplomatic contacts should be made with mainland China. In his homily in Hong Kong in 1970 he said that he felt the living presence of the seven hundred million Chinese, and that 'Christ is the loving Redeemer of China too'. All these moves were in line with Pope Paul's policy of being ready to try anything – even at the risk of rebuffs and failure – in order to transform the *de facto* interdependence of the nations of the world into an ordered and *de jure* interdependence.

Only a few elements of Pope Paul's *Westpolitik* can be mentioned here. Western Europe posed pastoral rather than political problems throughout the pontificate. But from the mid-seventies Mgr Benelli was authorized to lend Vatican support to greater European integration. Becoming Archbishop of Florence and Cardinal in 1977, he was well placed for this task. The theory was that the tighter the bonds which bound the E.E.C. countries together, the less would be the impact of communist participation in government, which was feared in France and expected in Italy itself. But Mgr Casaroli continued to speak of Europe in terms broader than the E.E.C., and was unwilling to write off Eastern Europe.

It was inevitable that the Pope's personal direction of affairs should have diminished towards the end of the reign. Latin American questions, for example, fell increasingly into the hands of Cardinal Baggio, President of the Pontifical Commission for Latin America. Ever since the Latin American Bishops (CELAM) meeting at Medellin in 1968 had launched their Church on the path of liberation, and proclaimed the need for 'radical social changes', the Church came under attack from increasingly authoritarian governments. Armed with what was known as 'the doctrine of national security', they began to use imprisonment and torture as ordinary instruments of government. In 1970 Pope Paul condemned the use of torture in Brazilian prisons: or rather, he referred to 'a certain great country' where 'cruel and inhuman tortures as a way of extorting confessions are to be roundly condemned'. 'Torture', he added, mitigating the blow, 'is spreading round the world like an epidemic.' Was it diplomatic restraint which determined this prudent ambiguity? No doubt. Brazil was to be warned but not branded.

A similar ambiguity clouded the passage in *Populorum Progressio* on the 'right to revolution'. It was little more than a re-statement of traditional doctrine, but the tone of voice or the stress could give it two contrasting meanings. Pope Paul had written:

> We know, however, that a revolutionary uprising – save where there is manifest, long-standing tyranny which would do great damage to fundamental personal rights and dangerous harm to the common good of the country – produces new injustices, throws more elements off balance

and brings on new disasters. A real evil should not be fought against at the cost of greater misery (31).

Theologians of liberation could and did stress the importance of the passage between dashes and maintained that they were indeed faced by 'manifest and long-standing tyranny' and 'structural injustice'; while governments could and did draw attention to the pessimism expressed in this passage about the likelihood of revolution ever improving anything. From this we can deduce that a 'diplomatic formulation' in the pejorative sense is one that tries to state both sides of a question and by trying to please everyone succeeds in pleasing no one. The efforts of Cardinal Baggio in the last years of the pontificate were devoted to ensuring that the 1978 meeting of the Latin American Bishops, this time due to meet at Puebla in Mexico, should not repeat the 'mistakes' of Medellin. In other words it should concentrate more on inner-Church matters and above all say nothing that would alarm governments.

Here we reach the limits of what diplomacy can do. It is tempting to suggest that there is a necessary tension between diplomacy and prophecy, between the task of securing good relations with states and the duty of denouncing injustice. It is fair to add that Pope Paul constantly tried to reduce that gap and to be a prophet of peace and justice – the condition of peace – among all men. In any case, his form of prophecy was less a matter of verbal declarations than of vivid lived parables that caught the imagination and made hope possible. He went to the Holy Land, source of Christian faith, and embraced Patriarch Athenagoras. He went to India and prayed with this poor but deeply religious people. In Kampala, Uganda, he went out of his way to speak of the Anglican martyrs. As he stepped from the plane on his arrival in Bogotá, Colombia, he astonished everyone by kissing the soil of Latin America. In Manila he was attacked by a mad painter. Faced with the United Nations, the world in miniature, he pleaded for peace. In the end, diplomacy, as he understood it and expounded it to the students of the Pontifical Academy in 1951, had nothing to do with Machiavellian cunning and *l'astuzia fortunata*: it was rather the expression of charity on the vastest possible scale. It is customary, and perhaps abusive, to contrast 'diplomatic' and 'pastoral' popes. Pope John Paul I frankly confessed his inexperience in international affairs. Pope John Paul II has made it clear that he sees diplomatic activity as part of the pastoral goal of the Church. Pope Paul left him a rich inheritance.

4

Count-down to the Conclave

*The personality of the pope, and the ideas he has, are
important factors in the onward movement of the Church:
but even in this field it is the masses who make history.*
Humanité, the French communist paper,
28 August 1978

The count-down to the conclave began on the day Pope
Paul died. This image was suggested by a useful chart
designed to help the staff of Vatican Radio. Let the day
the Pope died be described as o and subsequent days indicated by a + sign. The funeral was set for +6 and with
it began the *Novemdiales* or nine days of mourning which
would last until +14. The conclave itself was soon fixed
for +20, the latest possible date: the significance of this
late date was not immediately apparent, and it produced
groans among reporters who had been rescued from the
Lambeth Conference or untimely torn from their summer
holidays at Saint Jean de Luz or Cape Cod. How long the
conclave would last was anyone's guess, but the pattern of
the two previous conclaves suggested that by about +30
the new pope would have been elected and crowned. In
fact Pope John Paul I was elected on +21 and 'inaugurated
his ministry as Supreme Pastor' on +29.

But the count-down to the conclave had really begun
much further back. As new cardinals were created at each
successive Consistory, commentators remarked that Pope
Paul was gradually building up the college that would elect
his successor. Many red hats (now merely of heraldic signifi-

cance) simply go with the job. Pope Paul had imaginatively
appointed Josef Ratzinger, a distinguished theologian, to
Munich and Basil Hume, a Benedictine Abbot, to Westminster: the only surprise when they became cardinals was
at the swiftness of the honour. Significance lay rather in
departures from precedent. When Stephen Kim, Archbishop
of Seoul, was made a cardinal in 1969, Pope Paul was said
to be striking a blow for the third world, strengthening
Kim in his struggles with President Park, and generally
making the college of cardinals more geographically representative. And the appointment of many African and Asian
cardinals gave the college a new and colourful appearance.
The 1978 conclave would be the biggest ever, with 111
electors, and the most geographically diversified. There
were 56 cardinals from Europe, among whom 27 Italians;
12 from Africa (compared with 2 in 1963); 13 from Asia
and Oceania (5 in 1963); 19 Latin Americans (11 in 1963);
and 11 North Americans (7 in 1963).

Pope Paul had certainly made the College of Cardinals
more representative of the geographical spread of Catholicism. But apart from that, it was difficult to find any
discoverable principle in his appointments other than a
general desire to preserve a balance between 'conservatives'
and 'progressives'. I use the terms to refer to those who were
(perhaps inwardly) suspicious about the Second Vatican
Council and those who welcomed it whole-heartedly as a
liberation. Thus Cardinal Jaime L. Sin of Manila was a
very different man from his princely predecessor, Cardinal
Santos, whose friendship with President Marcos had been
embarrassingly close. Sin was prepared to denounce the use
of torture and arbitrary arrests, and protested to the
President when a decree was passed which would have
prevented clergy from engaging in social work. The decree
was withdrawn. Sin was clearly progressive. But on the other
hand the appointment of Corrado Bafile, formerly nuncio
in West Germany where he had been caught red-handed
trying to secure the dismissal of Bishop Wilhelm Kempf of
Limburg (his letter suggesting that the Bishop could easily

give grounds of health as the reason for his resignation was leaked) seemed a distinctly unnecessary reward for dubious services rendered. Bafile was clearly conservative. The appointment of Giovanni Benelli to Florence made more sense. For years all attacks on Benelli – they were numerous and often ill-founded – had been met with the reply that Pope Paul found him indispensable in the management of the Roman Curia. But then, suddenly, in June 1977 the indispensable manager was dispensed with and sent to take over the important diocese of Florence. As mere *sostituto* he would not have taken part in the conclave. As a cardinal enriched with 'pastoral experience', he would be an important figure. The future was being prepared.

There was another way in which the conclave was being prepared. It was a common journalistic device (regularly used by Alain de Penaster of the French magazine *L'Express*) to present Synods from 1974 onwards as a 'dress rehearsal' for the forthcoming conclave. Great attention was paid to the election to the Synod Secretariat. There was something in this idea. But it ignored some vital distinctions between the two contests. The electoral body at the Synod was made up more of bishops than of cardinals: they were electing nine people – the other three were nominated by the Pope – for somewhat shadowy responsibilities rather than one for awesome and precise responsibilities; and popularity at the Synod could depend on superficial criteria – the man had made a striking speech – which would not impress the more hard-headed College of Cardinals. It was noteworthy that Albino Luciani, Patriarch of Venice, had never made a headline-grabbing speech at a Synod. However, it could at least be reasonably argued that the Synod, together with participation in Vatican Congregations, meant that the cardinals at the next conclave would know each other better than ever before. It also meant that the curial cardinals would to some extent lose the advantage of being a tightly-knit body who were the only people who could claim to have an overall view of the Church and its needs. The cardinals in conclave would not meet as total strangers.

That was another way in which the conclaves of 1978 would be different.

The pope cannot designate his successor. But in a long pontificate he can set up the College that will elect him. And since mortality affects popes as much as other men, one never quite knows just how close a conclave might be. One is always only a heart-beat away. The successive measures by which Pope Paul had recommended diocesan bishops and curial cardinals to retire at 75, and excluded cardinals over eighty from the conclave, were taken at a time when he might reasonably have thought that he would not reach the fatal age. And when he lived on, he was faced with a dilemma which some of the over-eighties did not hesitate to put to him. Cardinal Alfredo Ottaviani, for instance, the baker's son from Trastevere, who was still alive at 89, had enquired why, if cardinals over eighty were thought incapable of electing a pope, a pope over eighty was considered capable of the daunting tasks of the pontificate. There were rumours that Pope Paul would have resigned, if he could have been confident that the cardinals would elect Sergio Pignedoli to succeed him; and at a later stage the favourite son or dauphin was said to be Giovanni Benelli, an idea that the Cardinal Archbishop of Florence did nothing to discourage. But all these suggestions came to nothing. Pope Paul did not resign: he died in harness.

But the conviction was growing in the Church that the election of a pope was too important a matter to be left to the College of Cardinals alone. Whereas conclaves up to the beginning of the twentieth century had to fear the intrigues of ambassadors in Rome and the veto of European princes – the Austrians were alleged to have vetoed Cardinal Rampolla in 1902 and thus unwittingly prepared the way for Pope St Pius X – the 1978 conclaves were exposed to the pressures of public opinion in the Church. It was not a matter of dictating to the cardinals who should be pope. It was rather, as Giancarlo Zizola argued in *Quale Papa?* (Borla, Rome, 1977), that the whole Church should be engaged in the discussion about what sort of pope was needed for what sort of Church in what sort of world. A group of American Catholics calling themselves, with intentional humour, the Committee for the Responsible Election of the Pope (CREP) seized this torch and made a plea for an open conclave in which everything would be above board. Unfortunately, the apostolic constitution of 1975, *Romano Pontifici Eligendo*, had already decreed that the next conclave would be – in theory at least – the most secret ever, and made special provision to counter bugging and other electronic devices. Later, as we shall see, CREP came to town.

Meanwhile, the formalities had to be observed. On +1 there was the first meeting of cardinals who happened to be in Rome in August. They met in the Sala Bologna on the third floor of the Apostolic Palace. There were fifteen of them, including the over-eighties who were allowed to attend these pre-conclave meetings which were known as General Congregations. As Dean of the College, 85-year-old Cardinal Confalonieri presided: the significance of that was also missed at the time. Here was a man who had been present at the 1922 conclave as secretary to Cardinal Achille Ratti who emerged – a surprise choice – as Pope Pius XI. He had also been Prefect of the Congregation of Bishops when Albino Luciani was made Bishop of Vittoria Veneto in 1958. He greatly enjoyed his presidential role and found it piquant that, though excluded from the conclave, he could still in some way affect its outcome. But on +1 he seemed to be overshadowed, literally and metaphorically, by the six-foot-four figure of Cardinal Jean Villot, the French Secretary of State. Villot was the most important exception to the rule, introduced by Pope Paul to give the new pope freedom of action, that all curial cardinals must automatically resign on the death of a pope. Not only that, but on 16 August 1970 Pope Paul had appointed him *camerlengo* or chamberlain, which meant that during the *sede vacante* period between two popes, he became the official keeper of the keys of Peter. He was the first ever non-Italian to hold the office of chamberlain, and only the second person in a hundred years to combine both offices. Since the last cardinal who had been both Secretary of State and chamberlain was Eugenio Pacelli in 1939, who went on to become Pius XII, that might have been considered a portent.

But it did not mean that Villot was a serious contender for the papacy. Italians alleged that he did not understand their tangled political situation, though he was shrewd enough to forecast that a referendum on divorce would result in a defeat for the Church. No one thanked him for being right. But on +1 he was in charge and summoned by telephone those cardinals who were in Rome. Day by day there were new arrivals – by +4 there were 43 and by +6 over a 100 – but Villot had committed a technical blunder: to be valid, the invitations to the General Congregation should have been in writing. It was Cardinal Pericle Felici who pointed out this lapse from protocol. Villot, not the most legalistic of men, gave a Gallic shrug and promised to write in future. He was constantly made the victim of a campaign of sniping innuendo. On +4 it was reported that he was incapable of finding the fisherman's ring with its pontifical seal. Pope Paul had left it at the back of a drawer, and given the choice between concluding that Pope Paul was absent-minded or that Villot was incompetent, the sources leaned towards the latter theory. Salt was rubbed into his wounds. In Florence, Cardinal Benelli had said in a radio interview: 'The Cardinal Secretary of State had purely formal relations with the Holy Father, while I saw him every day.' It was enough to make a saint or a strong man weep, but Villot plodded on with his task of preparing first the funeral and then the conclave.

Meanwhile various pressure groups were submitting the cardinals to an unwanted barrage of advice and exhortation. I will briefly describe three of them, simply for their representative value. They were part of the story of the conclave. For convenience they can be labelled the intransigent right, liberals of the centre and the radical left.

The intransigent right was splendidly represented in Rome by the Abbé François Ducand Bourget, curé of the Church of St Nicholas-du-Chardonnet in Paris, which has been 'occupied' by supporters of Archbishop Lefebvre since March 1977. Dapper, apple-cheeked and upright although eighty-two years old, he had made his way to Rome despite strikes by French air traffic controllers. Unlike many of his kind, he has the saving grace of humour. 'If I were elected pope,' he told Alain Woodrow of *Le Monde*, 'it would be one of the greatest miracles of all time.' His greatest objection to the conclave was the exclusion of the over-eighties. 'It's the first step towards euthanasia,' he said, 'and is in effect a sort of moral euthanasia.' However, he did not quite draw the conclusion of Lefebvre himself who had declared that he would 'refuse in advance a pope who was elected by a conclave which excluded the over-eighties'. According to him, the conclave would be invalid because of this radical departure from tradition. This rejection in advance was tactically a bad mistake on Lefebvre's part. For if part of his somewhat confused case was that Pope Paul had been personally responsible for the deviations into which the Church had fallen – by giving too ready an ear to Marxist and Masonic infiltrators – then a new pope, any new pope, ought to have given him at least a chance to seek for reconciliation and possibly even recognition. His statement showed that he did not really want reconciliation.

But it put pressure on the conclave in a rather curious way. With 111 electors, the number of votes required to win was 75 – two-thirds plus one. Since there were 16 cardinals over eighty, a candidate who saw his votes mounting up could reasonably ask for another ballot just to ensure that he had two-thirds plus one, plus two-thirds of sixteen. In this way he would be in a juridically unassailable position should Lefebvre wish to challenge his election. For although the voting was supposed to be secret and dire oaths were sworn, few thought that the figures would long remain unknown. But Lefebvre and Ducand Bourget were not the only voices of the intransigent right. Also fighting the wrong battle in the last ditch was an Italian organization called *Civiltà Cristiana*. One of these defenders of Christian civilization rushed up to Cardinal Basil Hume the day before the conclave and handed him a leaflet. He passed it on to his secretary and asked what it said. Mgr George Leonard reported that it said, 'Elect a Catholic Pope'. 'What cheek!', replied Cardinal Hume. 'Do they think I am going to vote for Dr Coggan?' Meanwhile the posters urging the cardinals to 'Elect a Catholic Pope' fluttered on the walls of Rome.

The criticism from the radical left took a rather different form. Among the visitors to Rome was Jean-Claude Besret, formerly prior of the Benedictine house at Boquen in Normandy. Tall, soberly dressed, still with a Benedictine haircut and the look of a tortured mystic, he told everyone who cared to listen that the papal election was little more than a farce. 'We are abundantly informed', he wrote in *Le Monde* (12 August 1978) 'about the past life and the funeral of the dead pope, but we are rigorously excluded from the choice of his successor.' 'By what right', he went on, 'is the pope chosen in so archaic a fashion and with such complete disregard for the people whom he is supposed to serve?' The fact that millions of people looked upon the pope as a spiritual leader and someone who could help them interpret the meaning of life required, he maintained, something more than the illusion of choice from among a pre-selected group. 'In the locked enclosure of the conclave', he declared, 'the psycho-drama of Christian alienation is being played out.' But after these grandiose declarations of principle, he found himself somewhat perplexed about how to reform the iniquitous system. He ruled out direct election by the people of Rome or by the whole Church, and instead opted for a vaguely sketched vision in which living Christian communities would somehow participate.

The American liberal suggestions were at first sight a little more practical. CREP thought that the people of God ought at least to know who the electors were and what their 'mind-set' was, and accordingly produced a book, *The Inner Elite* (Sheed, Andrews and McMeel, Inc., Kansas City, 1978). Unfortunately, its potted biographies were so riddled with errors, misleading statements and faulty deductions that the work, though eagerly perused by desperate journalists, was less useful than it might have been. One read, for instance that Cardinal Corrado Ursi, Archbishop of Naples, was born in July 1931 (p. 235). That would have made him, at 47, by far the youngest of the cardinals. It would also have meant that he was appointed Bishop of Nardo at the unusually early age of 20. In fact, Cardinal Ursi was born on 26 July 1908. Cardinal Wojtyla, we were told, took part in the 1959 Synod (p. 172), a remarkable feat, since it had not then been established. Yet since there were no competitors, *The Inner Elite* flourished.

Nothing daunted, CREP organized a press conference in the Hotel Columbus on the day after Pope Paul's funeral. Jim Andrews of CREP spoke first and explained that the purpose of his organization was 'to do away with the secrecy of the conclave, and to allow the world community to see the actual political process that is going on, and to participate in it'. The idea was to let the world know just who were these 'faceless, nameless' men who were about to elect the next pope. Since every newspaper in the non-communist world had been carrying photographs of the likely contenders throughout the previous week, the suggestion that they were faceless was wide of the mark: their faces had been almost too much with us.

But the purpose of the press conference was not to sell copies of *The Inner Elite*. It was to introduce Fr Andrew Greeley who, Andrews said with suitable awe, had written over eighty books. This feat was once explained by someone who remarked that 'Fr Greeley has never had an unpublished thought in his life'; and when he wrote a book called *Sexual Intimacy*, a reviewer in *America* added that now he had never had an unpublished fantasy in his life. However, on this sunny August morning he was intent upon sketching out his 'job description' of a pope. Here is part of it:

It does not matter whether the pope is a curial cardinal or a non-curial cardinal, nor whether he is Italian or not, nor whether he is of the first, second or third world; nor whether he is intellectual or non-intellectual, nor whether he is a diplomat or a pastor, progressive or moderate, efficient administrator or lacking in administrative experience; whether he is a liberation theologian or a traditional theologian, or what stands he takes or has taken on political issues facing the world.

Doubtless someone in the papal entourage must be an efficient administrator, someone must be a theologian, someone must be a diplomat, someone must understand Italy, someone must be sensitive to the third world, someone must know how the Roman Curia runs and how it can be brought under control; but it is not necessary for the pope to have any of these abilities. For men with such talents can be found; they are not required for the top position in the Catholic Church.

At the present critical time of its history, faced with the most acute crisis, perhaps, since the Reformation, and dealing with a world in which both faith and community are desperately sought, the papacy requires a man of holiness, a man of hope, a man of joy. A sociologically oriented job description of the pope, in other words, must conclude that the Catholic Church needs as its leader a holy man who can smile.

Few would wish to quarrel with the conclusion, remarkably prophetic in its way, that the pope should be 'a holy man who can smile'. If Greeley had not got in first with the phrase, Cardinal Terence J. Cooke of New York might have said it himself.

In the subsequent discussion, Greeley denied that his job description was merely the antithesis of a certain 'image' of Pope Paul, averred that he would not be opposed to a woman pope and said that 'a papessa could not make more of a mess of the Church than we men have over the last 1900 years. *Viva la papessa*!' Even more curious was his answer to a question about why American Catholics had been so perturbed by *Humanae Vitae*, while largely ignoring

Populorum Progressio, Pope Paul's encyclical on social questions. Greeley's answer was that 'if an organization fails to communicate, it must assume that *it* has failed, not that the *people* have failed'. But the 'sociology of communications' suggests that it is a two-way process involving the messenger, his message and the recipient. If American Catholics were inclined to disregard *Populorum Progressio*, this may partly have been because they felt challenged as members of the richest nation in the world. To ignore it was a defence against guilt about the third world. After his press conference, Professor Greeley could be seen pacing the streets of Rome, muttering into his pocket tape-recorder and complaining that the Italians did not understand the sociological approach.

A more coherent set of proposals was contained in an 'Open Letter to the Conclave' signed by a group of theologians associated with the review *Concilium* (full text in *The Tablet*, 19 August 1978, p. 811). They started from the premise that the Catholic Church, because it is the largest, can make a special contribution towards Christian unity. The pope should therefore be a man open to the world, a spiritual guide, an authentic pastor, a brother in collegiality, an ecumenical mediator, a genuine Christian. He must keep a critical eye on the Church and society, and be open to 'the signs of the times and the changed mentality of people today'. He must have the courage to inspire others to courage, be a source of authority without being authoritarian, and commit himself for 'the repressed and underprivileged'. Parts of the Open Letter read like an *exercise de style*. However, the authors made one point of great importance, since it linked up with the Lutheran-Catholic dialogue mentioned in the Appendix. The papacy should be seen, they wrote, 'as a primacy of service within Christianity, which should be renewed in the spirit of the Gospel and exercised in favour of Christian liberty'. The pope must further 'set an example of Christian disponibility by removing the disciplinary or dogmatic obstacles to unity and by promoting co-operation with the World Council of

Churches.' They also hoped that the pope would 'accept the Synod of Bishops not simply as an advisory body but as a responsible, decision-making organ of the Church', that he would review the Vatican diplomatic service and give more power to episcopal conferences and diocesan councils. It was a formidable shopping-list.

The pressure groups deserve a mention because they reflected, as in a distorting mirror, some of the forces that were at work within the conclave itself. One could distinguish four main tendencies among the cardinals, depending on their analysis of the present state of the Church and their assessment of the pontificate of Pope Paul. They could be placed on a spectrum going from right to left.

Cardinal Pericle Felici, who had been Secretary General of the Council and subsequently responsible for the revision of the Code of Canon Law, was a good representative of the attitude of the conservatives. Pope Paul, they believed, had endangered the heritage of the Church by his vacillations. He had made, for instance, a tactical mistake on the question of birth-control. Before his long-awaited pronouncement, he had given the impression that the question was open and that he did not know his own mind. 'How easy it is to study,' he once said as the bulky dossiers piled up on his desk, 'how hard to decide.' In this way he hinted at the possibility of change which, orchestrated by the media, soon became the likelihood of change. But then, to dash it all, he published *Humanae Vitae* which confirmed the traditional view, thus ensuring the worst of all worlds. The conservative critics claimed that the same blunder had been made over the ordination of married men – a topic aired at the 1974 Synod – and the ordination of women, on which a special commission had been working. In each case the stable door was locked after the horses had bolted.

They concluded their catalogue of woe by drawing attention to the number of priests who have abandoned the ministry, the number of religious who have returned to the lay state, the disarray of the laity, and the relative success obtained by Archbishop Lefebvre who had exploited nostalgia for the Church as it once was: a firm rock against which the waves of the world lashed in vain. Flirting with ecumenism had weakened the sense of Catholic identity, and talking with Marxists had turned the Church, in some places, into an ally of the revolution. 'Authority abhors a vacuum', Cardinal Felici had told Dr Philip Potter when he visited the 1974 Synod. Felici would be the king-maker of this group and their likely candidates would be Cardinal Sebastiano Baggio, Prefect of the Congregation of Bishops, or Cardinal Giuseppe Siri, Archbishop of Genoa.

The second school of thought was reasonably happy with Pope Paul's pontificate. This attitude was found among many U.S. cardinals. They felt that Pope Paul was a good and tortured man doing an absolutely impossible job. He had managed to avoid open schism in the Church, and that was a considerable achievement. The next pope would have to continue his balanced policy of implementing the Council without excess. So continuity – if possible with a smile – was what was needed. The Church does not progress by turning somersaults. The likely king-maker was Cardinal Giovanni Benelli, Archbishop of Florence, who at 57 was too young to be considered a candidate; and the suggested candidate, Cardinal Sergio Pignedoli, who had once shared a flat with Pope Paul, been his auxiliary Bishop in Milan, and would provide a genial form of continuity with his friend.

The third force in the conclave could be called 'European progressive', though it did not include all Europeans and did not exclude the three Canadian cardinals. It was represented by Cardinal Jan Willebrands, Archbishop of Utrecht in the Netherlands and President of the Secretariat for Christian Unity; by Cardinal Franz König, Archbishop of Vienna and President of the Secretariat for Non-believers; and by Cardinal François Marty of Paris. Cardinal Léon-Joseph Suenens of Malines-Brussels had lapsed from this group after discovering the charismatic movement, and Cardinal Basil Hume of Westminster was its most youthful recruit. Their views were not too far distant from the Open

Letter of the *Concilium* theologians. They took ecumenism seriously, and expected it to get somewhere. They wanted the Church to be positive rather than fearful. They did not regard the Council as the cause of chaos in the Church but as an opportunity for renewal. But this group was numerically weak in the conclave, and did not have any organization. The name of Cardinal Willebrands was put forward by the distinguished French Dominican, Yves-Marie Congar. The last Dutch Pope, Adrian VI, was a reforming pope who reigned only a year and a half (1522–3). He was also the last non-Italian pope. If he had lived longer he might have helped to avert the tragic split of the Reformation. It would be appropriate for another Dutch pope finally to heal those lingering wounds in the Body of Christ. But Congar was not in the conclave, and his suggestion was wishful thinking.

In any case, the 'European progressives' were outflanked by the more numerous third world cardinals. At least sixteen out of the twenty Latin Americans were not unsympathetic to the theology of liberation; and though they had little support from Africa, Asia could come to their aid with men like Cardinal Joseph Cordeiro of Karachi and Cardinal Stephen Kim of Korea. Their view of the Church was coloured by their own situations. Cardinal Evaristo Arns, Archbishop of São Paolo, Brazil, comes from a diocese of over six million people. Half of them have been uprooted from their traditional homes in the last three years. Many are living in shanty towns. Such experiences gave the third world cardinals a different set of priorities. They were not opposed to ecumenism, but it did not seem to them so urgent as the problems of poverty, hunger and despotic military governments. Any idea that the Lefebvre affair was an important issue would have seemed to them merely risible. For them, the Church had to be the Church of the poorest, not because this was good for its image, but because it is in the poorest that Christ is encountered today. They were often labelled 'communist' by their governments who, armed with the doctrine of 'national security', were able to crush all opposition. The timidities of Vatican diplomacy seemed to them to get in the way of the duty of prophecy. Cardinal Aloisio Lorscheider, Archbishop of Fortaleza, Brazil, and President of the Latin American Bishops' Conference (CELAM), was the natural leader of this group. It remained for them to find a candidate.

Two names that were difficult to place on the spectrum and which rarely appeared in lists of *papabili* were those of Cardinal Albino Luciani, Patriarch of Venice, and Cardinal Karol Wojtyla, Archbishop of Krakow. It would be easy to write history with hindsight and to show that their eventual emergence was logical and, indeed, almost inevitable. But I wanted to remain true to the perceptions available, both to cardinals and observers, *at the time*. In any case, a papal election is a very odd process. It is quite unlike any other election, and the smoke-filled rooms of Cook County, Chicago, were not an illuminating parallel. In most elections, the candidates hope to win, present would-be attractive programmes to that end, and solicit support. In a conclave, candidates are supposed to be dragged unwillingly to the pontifical throne, they are not encouraged to present programmes, and they are positively forbidden to make pacts in advance. Moreover the Holy Spirit brings an added element of uncertainty into the process. Yet the ordinary laws of group dynamics still applied to the 111 cardinals as they prepared for the first conclave of 1978, and they were not inactive. What they were doing will be the subject of the next chapter.

5

Plots and the Holy Spirit

> *So we'll live,*
> *And pray, and sing, and tell old tales, and laugh*
> *At gilded butterflies, and hear poor rogues*
> *Talk of court news; and we'll talk with them too,*
> *Who loses and who wins, who's in, who's out;*
> *And take upon's the mystery of things,*
> *As if we were God's spies.*
>
> Shakespeare, *King Lear*, Act V, scene 3

Pope Paul had hoped and intended that the conclave would be a place of prayer and quiet and that it would 'have the character of a sacred retreat' (*Romano Pontifici Eligendo*, No. 42). The same document expressly forbade 'any form of pact, agreement, promise or other commitment of whatever kind which could oblige them to give or not give their vote to a certain person or persons' (*ibid.*, No. 82). However, the cardinals were allowed to 'exchange views', something that, on reflection, it would be difficult altogether to prevent. These were the parameters of the conclave: it was to be a spiritual event, but it was made up of human beings. There were thus two ways of distorting what was actually happening. The first was to make the preparations for the conclave so sublime, so spiritual, so Spirit-assisted, that it became unintelligible in human terms. The second was to present it in such a political and unspiritual way that it became a matter of wheeler-dealing and, once again, unintelligible, this time in divine terms.

As an illustration of the first way of distorting the pre-conclave proceedings, one cannot do better than take an article written by Ersilio Tonini, Bishop of Ravenna and

Cervia, which was published in *Osservatore Romano* (19
August 1978: it had previously appeared in *Avvenire*, the
Catholic daily). Bishop Tonini began by deploring the fact
that Ladbroke's, the London book-makers, had been offer-
ing odds on the conclave. 'This is unworthy', he said, 'of
the tact of the English.' Next he denounced fantastic journalistic speculations which had suggested, for example, that
there was an alliance between West German cardinals and
some of their client cardinals in Latin America, in order
to stop a 'move to the left'. This was a routine *Osservatore
Romano* tactic: first insist on secrecy, and then denounce
those whose speculations hasten to fill in the void. But Bishop
Tonini's principal concern was to raise the discussion of the
conclave to a higher level. 'It is not true', he wrote dis-
concertingly, 'that the main protagonist in the election of a
pope is the college of cardinals.' That might cause eyebrow-
raising. Why, then, had they so expensively gathered in
Rome? Bishop Tonini explained: 'The real protagonist is
the Other, whose presence and involvement transform the
event completely and make it a community act of the
Church.' By the 'Other' he meant the Holy Spirit who thus
became the 112th and most important member of the
conclave.

He went on to make a perfectly valid theological point:
'By this election the cardinals do not confer or transfer power
to the one they elect: they merely designate him. Christ
himself is needed to confer these powers.' Then he quoted
St Augustine: 'Christ has reserved power to himself: to us
he has given the ministry of service.' Sacramental theologians like Edward Schillebeeckx have pointed out, however, that it is a mistake to suppose that ministry in the
Church must come either wholly from above or wholly
from below. The Holy Spirit is at work in the conclave as
in the Church, and though his promptings always have to
be tested, the mission comes *from* Christ but *through* the
community, which in this case was the College of Cardinals.
The human mediation is indispensable.

The notion that the Holy Spirit was the prime mover in

the conclave was graphically illustrated by a painting which *Osservatore della Domenica*, the Sunday version of *Osservatore Romano*, reproduced for the edification of its readers. It was by Sebastiano Ricci (1659–1734) and can be seen in the civic museum of Piacenza. Ricci relegated the cardinals in their red birettas into obscurity; the foreground was entirely dominated by a brilliant flash of intense light, out of which emerged a dove which alighted on the tiara, symbol of papal power.

That the *grande elettore*, the most important elector, would be the Holy Spirit, became a cliché of the conclave. It was something cardinals could use to deflect awkward questions. It became the ecclesiastical equivalent of 'No comment'. One sighed for a linguistic philosopher, of undoubted faith, who would make sense of this discourse on the Holy Spirit. He would want, no doubt, to examine not so much its meaning as its function. How did it operate in ordinary pre-conclave usage? Its main function was to ensure advance approval for whoever would be elected. It suggested that 'It didn't really matter who was elected', since the Holy Spirit was in charge. It made the idea of a bad or unsuitable pope impossible (though no one could deny that there have been bad and unsuitable popes – a long time ago). And after the election it would act as the official divine ratification of what had been done. There is a valid use of Spirit-talk, as we shall see. But in the pre-conclave period it was often used abusively and mystifyingly. In any case, in the context of the conclave, it had never meant inaction or passivity. So assiduous was the French Ambassador, Pellegrino Rossi, at the 1846 conclave, that he was known as '*le comte du Saint-Esprit*'.

A similar point was forcibly made by Cardinal Giuseppe Siri in his sermon on +7. This was one of the *Novemdiales* Masses that were celebrated in St Peter's before the altar of the throne. His text was Matthew 14: 23–33 which relates how Peter walked on the water and began to sink when he thought of himself more than of Christ. Cardinal Siri's homily contained the following passage:

The cause of this miracle was the divine power: but divine
omnipotence, though it can do everything, leaves to every
creature its share of freedom. It does him the honour of
making him a co-cause. Human responsibility remains.
From this point of view, I think I have a duty to remind
my venerable brothers of the sacred college of the task
that is before them and which they cannot elude by
saying, 'This is what the Holy Spirit thinks.' Nor should
they abandon themselves, without toil and suffering, to
their first impulse or to unreasonable suggestions.

It was difficult to know the precise danger against which
Cardinal Siri, a well-known conservative, was warning his
brother cardinals. Certainly he was mistrustful of too facile
Spirit-talk. But, beyond that, did he fear that the cardinals
would go hot-headedly for a third world pope to please the
groundlings of the media? Or was he afraid that the conclave
would be borne along on a surge of charismatic enthusiasm
which would be comforting in the short run but damaging
in the long term? I cannot answer these questions. But
certainly Cardinal Siri went into the conclave expecting a
long, hard slog. 'It is like being buried alive', he said, after
surveying the conclave accommodation on +18.

Cardinal Siri was at least frank. The shocking paradox
of the situation was that some of those who were most ready
to talk of the Holy Spirit for public consumption were the
very ones who in private had a purely 'political' approach
to the conclave. Here I am going to report a conversation
with someone I propose to call, to save his neck, Mgr
Ossobuco. He judged the conclave entirely in terms of
political strategy. Cardinal Stefan Wyszinski, he claimed,
would receive a significant sympathy vote as a great defender
of the faith and a resolute anti-communist. Both the West
German and the East European cardinals would want to
know more about the deleterious effects of the Vatican's
Ostpolitik. Like President Carter, they believed that a
'tougher line' on human rights would produce more solid
results. There had been too much kow-towing to Com-

munists. Dialogue had got nowhere. In fact, wherever Ossobuco looked, he saw the total failure of the policy of dialogue pursued by Pope Paul. Cardinal Pignedoli could be ruled out as a serious candidate, not simply because of his gaffe at the Christian–Moslem Seminar in Tripoli, when in the closing stages he had allowed Colonel Gadhafi to slip in a resolution which condemned 'Zionism as racism', but because the African bishops south of the Sahara were deeply worried by the Moslem proselytizing offensive that was being directed against their peoples. It so happened that I had attended Colonel Gadhafi's seminar, and believed that Cardinal Pignedoli's famous gaffe, if it existed at all, had been exaggerated out of all proportion; and had noted that the further one got away from the cauldron of the Middle East, the better were Christian–Moslem relations.

Toughness all round and less dialogue was Ossobuco's remedy for the Church's ills. He was prepared to make no concession whatever to the idea that the papacy had changed, and cavalierly ignored the fact that the world had changed. It was as though ordinary Catholics throughout the world merely provided the cannon fodder for some vast strategic plan, the aim of which was to protect the institution. Ossobuco, evidently, was a real die-hard. His judgement on Cardinal Hume, which he erroneously attributed to the majority of the cardinals, was severe. I will report it in all its distressing harshness: 'Cardinal Hume? They don't know who he is. After all, he's a new boy. All they know about him is that he doesn't know what the Church's position on abortion is, and that he would give communion to Anglicans.' Since – to borrow Greeley's phrase – the ratio of Ossobuco's talking to his listening was about 20:1, it would have been useless to explain to him that at least the cardinals knew that Cardinal Hume had been a Benedictine Abbot, which in itself told them a good deal. Or that his remarks on inter-communion at the Anglican Synod had simply noted that there was pressure for it. Or that his 'hesitation' on abortion came in an early television interview with Ludovic Kennedy, who had presented him with a compli-

cated case of conscience to which he replied that he would
need more time to think that through. What came through
to most viewers as painstaking honesty had been travestied
into flabbiness on fundamental moral principles. It was
useless, too, to explain to Ossobuco that Cardinal Hume's
genuine search for God and his willingness to say that he
did not know when he did not, had done more to commend
the Church than the confident certainties of his predecessor,
Cardinal Heenan, who once said to Malcolm Muggeridge
that he had 'never had a serious doubt in his life'. Happily,
Ossobuco was not in the conclave. But he made me feel
the truth of Mgr Ronald Knox's remark on why he had
never been to Rome: 'The bad sailor should not go down
into the engine-room.'

Spirit-talk can be valid, but only under certain conditions.
When it is used to elude questions or to legitimate a course
of action on which I am engaged, it is misused; but if it
is accompanied by openness to the surprising Holy Spirit
and a readiness to accept his promptings, then it may be
valid. But it still has to be tested. Cardinal Hume put the
whole matter in perspective when he preached in his church
of San Silvestro on + 17, the Wednesday before the conclave:

> Rarely does God intervene in human affairs with that
> immediacy which would make momentous and grave
> decisions so much clearer, and response to them so much
> easier. His delicacy of touch is to pay man the compliment
> of being his collaborator. It is through human instruments,
> then, that the divine purpose is worked out and achieved.

So Cardinal Hume prepared himself for the conclave by
meditating on the Council's constitution *On The Church*. He
had also taken along George Eliot's *Middlemarch*, but found
it heavy going and was relieved to find back numbers of
Punch in a corner of the English College.

But not all the cardinals were so innocently engaged. The
nine sermons of the *Novemdiales* were given – with the exception of one by the Armenian Patriarch – by members

of the Roman Curia. Some of them were unexceptionally banal. But the sermons given by Confalonieri, Felici and Caprio, presented a picture of Pope Paul in which his agreement with their views was brought out. They made no mention of *Ecclesiam Suam*, the encyclical of dialogue, or of *Populorum Progressio*, the encyclical of social development, or even of *Humanae Vitae*, the encyclical which aroused dissent. For them the high point of the pontificate was the 'Credo of the People of God'. It was described by Confalonieri as 'one of the principal achievements of the pontificate'; Felici said it was 'an important act of the pontificate'; and on 19 August it was the turn of Giuseppe Caprio who said that 'Pope Paul was above all a man of faith, who gave us the "Credo of the People of God"'. In other words, in this curially edited version of the life and work of Pope Paul, he was presented solely as the pope of doctrinal firmness. Not everyone who remembered what the 'Credo of the People of God' was, shared this enthusiasm for it. Issued on 29 June 1968, and rather lost sight of in the storm which raged around *Humanae Vitae* just a few weeks later, it had been received by theologians with dismay. It contained whole passages from the Council of Trent on original sin – transmitted not by imitation but by propagation – and spoke warmly of angels and transubstantiation. It was not that the theologians disagreed with what it said: the trouble was rather that the Credo seemed to be content with mere repetition and to reject in advance all the attempts that had been made to find a contemporary language for faith. One professor at the Jesuit Gregorian University commented sadly: 'We can now close down all theological institutes and simply send for the record from Rome.'

These sermons, then, were the opening salvoes in a campaign to urge the conclave to elect a pope of conservative theological views. And the heritage of Pope Paul, which was much richer, was narrowed down to suit their case. Cardinal Ugo Poletti had the right to give two sermons on successive days, the first as Archpriest of the Basilica of St Peter's and the second as Vicar of the diocese of Rome. On 16 August his sermon was an elegant oratorical exercise on the four basilicas of Rome. St Mary Major, originally built in memory of the Council of Ephesus, which had defined Mary as the Mother of God, was the quietest and most devout of the basilicas. St John Lateran was a reminder that the pope was primarily the Bishop of Rome. St Paul's Without the Walls evoked the missionary dimension of the Church. And St Peter's – ah! St Peter's! – was described in rolling Ciceronian periods as 'this astonishing basilica, which by its vastness, openness, solemnity and sacred quality, could not better display the universality, the fraternity and the liberty of sons in the paternal house'. Pilgrims had come here from the earliest times, and all felt at home in their father's house. Ecumenism was mentioned, in passing, but it was ecumenism of the return-to-Rome variety. No one had ever told him, apparently, that the triumphalism of St Peter's (and all those saints on its façade who seem to be saying, said H. V. Morton, 'We've got it in the bag') was offensive to some Christians. The late Archbishop Thomas D. Roberts, formerly Archbishop of Bombay, used to say: 'Whenever I look at St Peter's, I think of indulgences and the Reformation.'

Cardinal Poletti's second sermon, on 17 August, was entirely devoted to Pope Paul's 'jealous love' of Rome. He said that 'in the cares and worries of his daily ministry as universal pastor, he never forgot the diocese of Rome'. Interestingly enough, Poletti reversed an old Roman rhetorical theme. It had been customary, if a little implausible, to speak of the diocese of Rome as exemplary for the rest of the Church. But, said Poletti, in the last years of the pontificate, Rome, with its violence, kidnappings and murders, became a microcosm of our troubled world. It was, so to speak, the world on the pope's doorstep. From being exemplary, Rome had become typical. Pope Paul's initiatives in writing to the Red Brigades and emerging from the Vatican to preside at the funeral of Aldo Moro were movingly evoked. Poletti told his hearers that at his final meeting with Pope Paul on 10 July the only topic of conversation had been Rome. They had discussed the pastoral plan for the diocese in the coming year. Its theme was: 'The role of the clergy in Rome, this suffering, changing city.' Non-Romans (in the strict, not the Anglican, sense) might have felt just a little excluded by all this Roman in-talk. The possibility of a third world pope receded a little further. The case for an Italian had been implicitly made.

But apart from this last point, which was strong, it could be said that the Curia had miscalculated by using the *Novemdiales* to suggest a pope of doctrinal rigour. For if the best that the Curia could offer was a rather unimaginative re-run of old and played out themes, then it was unlikely that a pope acceptable to the conclave would emerge from it.

This truth was already apparent to Cardinal Giovanni Benelli whose chess-playing mind had grasped two important points: the cardinals were unlikely to want a pope from the Roman Curia, and though they might toy with the dramatic idea of a pope from the third world, it would not be difficult to persuade them that, once again, an Italian was needed because of the needs of the diocese of Rome and the complexities of the Italian political situation. The next pope, therefore, would have to be an Italian residential cardinal. He would also have to be 'a pastoral bishop'. The choice of candidates was thus very restricted. The list came down to Cardinal Salvatore Pappalardo of Palermo, Sicily; Cardinal Corrado Ursi of Naples; Cardinal Giuseppe Siri of Genoa; and, finally, Cardinal Albino Luciani, Patriarch of Venice. But given this roster of names, the choice made itself. Pappalardo was too young at 59 and had been too preoccupied combating the *mafia*; Ursi was holy but rather provincial; while Siri was so intransigently right-wing that a consensus could never gather round him. That left Luciani who, moreover, had been well-placed in Venice for ecumenical contacts – the Secretariat for Christian Unity was pleased at the way he had made his palace and its generous hospitality available to them; at 65 he seemed exactly the right age; he was, in the words of the late Cardinal Giacomo Lercaro, 'holy and learned'; he clearly disdained the trappings of authority – he had refused to enter his diocese in the magnificent gondola used by his predecessors, including Roncalli; and he had an attractive writing and speaking style that would make him popular. Moreover, over the last year, Benelli had come to know him well: they were in the same regional conference of Italian Bishops. He was a most promising candidate.

Nothing in the previous paragraph can be proved: and although it contains nothing discreditable, it would no doubt be indignantly denied. But on 23 August I met by chance an important Vatican official – he had better be called *Sotto Voce* – who was used to distinguishing fact from speculation and had rarely been proved wrong. Compared with *Sotto Voce*, Ossobuco was an irrelevant clod-hopper. *Sotto Voce* confirmed that Luciani was indeed Benelli's candidate, and this was at a time when no one outside the conclave had even mentioned Luciani. 'Benelli', he said, 'cannot vote for any of the favoured candidates. Baggio and Siri will be put forward by the Curia, and Pignedoli will have some support. But Benelli will concentrate his votes on Luciani.' This was an important clue. But *Sotto Voce* left it unclear, and perhaps did not know, whether this was a preliminary move, designed to secure a bargaining counter in subsequent ballots, or whether it was Benelli's decisive move. I inclined to the second view, on the grounds that Benelli realized perfectly well that he was too young to be a candidate – the last pope elected in his mid-fifties had been Pio Nono, and his long pontificate became an embarrassment to the Church – and because, anyway, he prefers the role of second in command or *éminence grise*. To avoid all misunderstanding I should add that ecclesiastical ambition differs from secular ambition: if a churchman wants promotion, the motive is not personal self-aggrandizement – it would be folly to seek high office for its own sake – but so that he can work for the good of the Church as he conceives it.

But – and here was a surprise – Cardinal Benelli left Rome for Florence on the evening of 16 August and stayed there until shortly before the conclave. Thus he adroitly removed himself from the foreground of the action, could not be observed (as others were) giving discreet lunches to fellow cardinals, and went about his ordinary pastoral duties as a good bishop should. On the Sunday before the conclave, 20 August, he was at the Santa Teresa prison in Florence to confirm a 25-year-old prisoner, Luigi Ruggieri. Journalists and photographers were there to record the event. The sermon, alas, somewhat marred the effect. 'Others', he told the inmates, 'live within four walls as you do, but they freely choose to do so, all their life long: they are called monks.' No one asked whether the prisoners found this a consoling thought. But the inference was that Benelli, far from plotting in cool corners of elegant Roman salons, had his mind on higher things. No doubt he had. But his hand could still be on the telephone. According to F. X. Murphy: 'In telephone calls from Florence to conservative electors, Benelli stressed Luciani's resolute opposition to communism in Italy, his strong defence of the Church's stand against divorce and abortion, and his traditionalist theology. In calls to third world bishops, he emphasized Luciani's working-class background and genuine care for the poor' (*Newsweek*, 11 September 1978). The constituency was gradually being built up.

Journalists, meanwhile, who knew nothing of what was going on, were getting increasingly frustrated. Every promising plot they thought they had uncovered was later denied. *Il Giorno* of 21 August reported in some detail a meeting said to have been held at the Colegio Pio Latino on the via Aurelia. The Latin American cardinals, minus their more obvious die-hards, were said to have written a letter to their fellow cardinals urging 'an open-minded candidate who would continue the work of Vatican II and appreciate the problems of the third world'. The next day, Cardinal Lorscheider denied that such a letter had ever been written, though it would have been in no way discreditable if it had. After all, something must have been talked about at table in the Colegio Pio Latino, and everyone was busy drawing up an Identikit portrait of the next pope.

The same 21 August, another Rome paper, *La Repubblica*, printed the text of a letter from Vittorio Cordero di Montezemolo, Italian Ambassador to the Holy See, in which the main *papabili* were analysed from the point of view of acceptability to the Italian government. The likely political attitudes of Cardinals Villot, Benelli, Gantin, Poletti, Pappalardo and Pignedoli were discussed. The next day the letter was said to have been 'only a private document for internal use' and it had no official status. Revelations having failed, there remained the last resort of interviews; but cardinals, who in any case had been studiously and scrupulously vague, now relapsed into silence. *La Repubblica*, however, did not give up trying and secured an interview with Fr Virgilio Levi, deputy editor of *Osservatore Romano*. Not that he was any wiser than anyone else. He predicted a long conclave and said: 'The names of Pignedoli, Baggio, Bertoli and Pironio have been very frequently mentioned, and certainly all of them have the necessary qualities; but one cannot exclude a surprise name such as that of Confalonieri' (24 August). That would indeed have been a surprise: the first 85-year-old to be elected in the history of the papacy. The last 80-year-old had been Clement X in 1670. We knew that the average expectation of life was increasing, but Don Levi's suggestion seemed a little far-fetched.

Journalistic frustration worked itself out in the customary professional manner: the energetic protest. There were three of them, one in Italian, one in English, and one – with a little help from the Jesuits – in Latin, which began with the ringing phrase *Dolore et Stupore*. The stupefaction and pain were caused by the facts that the Vatican Press Office proposed to close down after two o'clock in the afternoon in the week preceding the conclave, that the provision of telephones was woefully inadequate, and above all because only five English-language reporters were to be allowed into the conclave area to see the apartments. The main protest, addressed to Fr Romeo Panciroli, Director of the Vatican Press Office, said:

While adhering fully to the parallel protest made by our Italian colleagues, we would like to point out that many of us have been brought here at great expense from different parts of the world in order to write about the conclave, and we will find it extremely difficult to justify the exclusion of most of us to our respective organizations.

We are also puzzled by the fact that fifteen years ago, all journalists who wanted to see the conclave area were allowed to do so and this time only a restricted group will be admitted. Surely this flies in the face of everything that the Holy See has been saying about social communications for the past several years.

This conjured up a vision of irate editors cabling speedliest: GET COLOUR ON CONCLAVE AREA STOP OR FIRED. It seemed very urgent that the world should know the exact height of the chimney, the exact shade of the carpet in the Sistine Chapel, and what the domestic arrangements were. My own proposal was that the English-speaking party should consist of five women, including a Dutchwoman because they were honorary English speakers, on the grounds that they would be better at testing beds and looking over plant. It was rejected by my peers. The official reason for the limitation of numbers was a concern for security: to have an army of journalists tramping through the conclave area, with its countless renaissance nooks and crannies, might have tempted someone to conceal a bugging device. But the protest was entirely justified, and to some extent effective. The Press Office stayed open longer, more telephones were hastily installed, and the group that inspected the conclave area was slightly enlarged. But these were minor victories, and brought no one any closer to the inscrutable proceedings of the pre-conclave: in default of hard news, the press was allowed to luxuriate in trivia.

The day the conclave began, 25 August, there was the Mass 'for the Election of a Pope' before the altar of the throne, beneath Bernini's golden window with its dove symbolizing the Spirit. The period of speculation was nearly over, and one became obscurely aware that the cardinals, and we along with them, were moving into an atmosphere of prayer. It was not, however, easy to get in, or at least to get near. Bearing a ticket borrowed from a French journalist, which impressed no one, I had to climb round a pillar and push my way into the tribune reserved for press photographers. One of them objected to me singing the antiphon *Mandatum novum do vobis* ('A new commandment I give you, that you should love one another'), so I briefly muttered something about Vatican II and participation. We gave each other the kiss of peace. The sense of moving gradually into the atmosphere of the Holy Spirit was partly due to the dignified simplicity that Cardinal Villot brought to the celebration of the Mass. His ten-minute homily was a straightforward exposition of John 15:9–11. He interpreted the words of Jesus, 'As the Father is with me, so I will be with you. Remain in my love', as addressed to the conclave which was about to gather in another 'upper room'. They were spiritually not alone. They would be sustained by the prayer of the Church. He quoted St Augustine on Peter's task as the *officium amoris*, a service of charity. 'Soon', he concluded, '*one* of us will be called to be the foundation of the visible unity of the Church, but *all* of us will be called to be united in charity.'

The Mass was over, and the cardinals made their way, two by two, down the aisle towards the sacristy. There were skirmishes with Vatican gendarmes at crush barriers. Rude remarks were exchanged (as Cardinal Poletti had said, it is 'the father's house'). Then the cardinals, having removed their mitres and vestments, returned individually up the aisle through the crowd. Some, like Cardinal Suenens and Cardinal Hume, looked grave and preoccupied, as though still searching for the vital clue. Others, like Cardinal Gordon Gray of Edinburgh and Cardinal Reginald Delargey of Wellington, New Zealand, exchanged greetings with the crowd. Delargey, who must surely be known as 'Reggie' to his friends, waved cheerfully and said, 'See you all on Monday'. Minor curial cardinals scattered impartial blessings as they went by. Then there was a sudden burst of applause for Cardinal Wyszinski, which was no doubt a political gesture inspired by the defenders of Christian civilization, *Civiltà Cristiana*. But the crowd caught the mood and began to applaud anyone they recognized. Cardinal Pignedoli looked thoughtful, and Cardinal Benelli passed by with the air of a relaxed and knowing cherub. The next time we saw them there would be 110 cardinals and one pope.

6

The August Conclave

*Any candidate who comes along with a conservative or a
progressive label must expect to be defeated. The next
pope cannot be the pope of a faction within the Church.
He will have to rule from the centre and be the servant
of unity.*

The Spectator, 29 July 1978

At least we know how the conclave began. Shortly after
4.30 p.m. on the afternoon of 25 August the cardinals
gathered in the Pauline Chapel which has frescoes by
Michelangelo of the crucifixion of St Peter and the conversion of St Paul. They were wearing red cassocks, white
surplices, the red shoulder cape known as the *mozzetta*, and
red birettas. Shepherded by Mgr Virgilio Noé, the papal
master of ceremonies, and preceded by the Sistine Chapel
choir singing the *Veni Creator*, they processed in reverse order
of seniority through the Sala Ducale, beneath Bernini's
theatrical cherubs, and into the Sistine Chapel itself. They
would have noticed the stove in the left-hand corner: its
celebrated chimney was surrounded by tubular scaffolding
to keep it away from the wall and so protect the frescoes.
A gentle ramp led into the Chapel proper, where the floor
had been raised to provide extra seating room. It was
covered with a fawn-coloured wool felt carpet. Cards marked
the fixed places at the two rows of long narrow tables that
faced each other across the Chapel. The chairs, covered in
red velvet, were straight-backed and not very comfortable.
The prayers over, Mgr Noé cried '*Extra omnes*' ('All out')
and the choir, altar servers and television crews departed.
The same cry was heard at the two revolving cylinders – a

large one for food in the cortile Pappagallo and a small one for very special correspondence which was in the cortile San Damaso – which for the duration of the conclave would be the only means of communication with the outside world, apart from a telephone for the emergency that never happened. The entrances were sealed with solid double wooden partitions. The cardinals were on their own.

There was no voting on that first evening. Instead, the cardinals had to sit through another reading of parts of the apostolic constitution, *Romano Pontifici Eligendo*, and in particular Nos. 55–61 on secrecy. Anyone discovered introducing 'technical instruments, of whatever kind, for the recording, reproduction or transmission of voices and images' (No. 61) would have been immediately expelled. No one was ejected, so one assumes that nothing was discovered. Then came the oath by which the cardinals swore to follow the apostolic constitution, defend the rights of the Holy See, refuse all secular vetoes on the election, and keep the whole affair secret. The precise wording on secrecy was not without interest in view of later events:

> Above all, we promise and swear to observe with the greatest fidelity and with all persons, including the conclavists, the secret concerning what takes place in the conclave or place of the election, directly or indirectly concerning the scrutinies; not to break this secret in any way, either during the conclave or after the election of the new Pontiff, unless we are given special faculty or explicit authorization from the same future Pontiff (No. 49).

This was sworn on the Gospels with each cardinal adding: 'So help me God and these Holy Gospels that I touch with my hand.'

Then, after a brief and somewhat redundant discourse from Cardinal Villot, as chamberlain, on the importance of the election and the need to bear in mind the good of the Church and nothing else, they were allowed to go to their rooms which were quaintly known as 'cells'. The oldest and most fragile were allowed to have cells near the Sistine Chapel and the Sala Borgia where meals were taken; the others had cells assigned by lot the previous day. There were great differences between them. Some were poky little offices tucked away in odd corners, with discoloured walls where pictures and charts had been removed. Their telephones were unplugged and dead. Others were lodged in vast Renaissance reception rooms, where the ceiling was forty feet high, and the cardinal, after putting out the chandelier for the night, would have to pick his way nimbly around vast tables and capacious sofas. Particularly splendid and inconvenient was the suite known as 'Cardinal Cicognani's apartment': Cicognani had been Secretary of State before Cardinal Villot, and the apartments have retained his name because Villot was unwilling to move into them. But whether in a dingy office or a marble hall, the equipment for the conclave was standardized and modest: a simple infirmary bed borrowed from the College of Propaganda Fidei; a red-shaded lamp by the bed that was too faint to read by; a wash-basin, soap (made by Donge of Paris) and kleenex; a bucket for slops; a writing-table with note-paper and an ashtray; a prie-dieu. But the dominant impression was one of gloom. Not only were the shutters firmly closed but the windows were locked and sealed so that no messages could be sent in code to friends outside. Cardinal Hume was to say afterwards: 'Many people could criticize the way a conclave is arranged, but it came to me that all these arrangements were symbolic – there was nothing between the cardinals and God. That seemed to me to be right.' But Cardinal Siri had said that it was like living in an airless tomb. A protracted conclave would have been intolerable.

For the great majority of cardinals it was their first conclave ever. Only eleven of them had taken part in a conclave before. Cardinal Timothy Manning of Los Angeles said that he felt 'like a schoolboy on his first day at school'. But anyone with a historical sense, as he went to sleep that first night, might have ruminated on the different patterns taken by conclaves. There seemed to be basically three. There was the swift, day-long conclave such as those of 1878 which elected Leo XIII, and 1939 which elected Pius XII: in both cases an 'obvious' candidate had taken an early lead and soon swept all before him. Another common pattern was that of deadlock followed by a compromise that was also a surprise. In 1922 there had been a double deadlock. First Gasparri and Merry del Val were evenly matched for five ballots; then for four more ballots the contest was between Gasparri and La Fontaine; and only when it became obvious that neither side would switch to the other did Achille Ratti gain momentum and get elected at the fourteenth ballot. The third pattern, finally, involved a pre-conclave favourite who nevertheless needed to overcome considerable opposition before he could be elected. This happened in 1958 when Pope John XXIII was elected and at the election of Pope Paul VI in 1963.

The 1963 conclave is worth considering in some detail because some of the actors were the same as in 1978, because thanks to the patient work of Giancarlo Zizola in *Quale Papa?* (Borla, Rome, 1977, pp. 160–172) the story can now be told, and also because Pope Paul's apostolic constitution, *Romano Pontifici Eligendo*, was partly inspired by a desire to avoid the 'mistakes' of 1963. The conclave began on 19 June and had a clear issue before it: should the work of John XXIII, who had captured the imagination of the world, be continued? Or should the lid be put back on the Pandora's Box of troubles that he had opened by summoning a Council? There were 80 electors, of whom 29 were Italian. Cardinal Montini was the leading candidate of those who wanted Pope John's policies of openness and renewal continued, and he gained about 30 votes in the first ballot. But others who agreed with the policy of continuity had proposed a different candidate, Cardinal Lercaro of Bologna, whose saintliness, simplicity and Franciscan-like poverty seemed closer to Pope John than the diplomatic and bureaucratic experience of Montini. Lercaro picked up about 20 votes. The conservative opposition to both was led by Cardinal

Ottaviani and Cardinal Siri. Their candidate, Antoniutti, also mustered about 20 votes, not enough to win, but enough to block Lercaro or Montini. By the fourth ballot on the evening of 20 June Montini had gathered up the Lercaro votes and was well in the lead, but he was still short of the 54 votes (two thirds plus one) that he needed.

Two things happened that evening. The first was dramatic and broke all the rules. Cardinal Testa was a man who always claimed that he would never have been a cardinal but for Pope John (hence his motto: *Sola gratia tua*). He stood up in the conclave and asked his two neighbours, Confalonieri and di Jorio, but in a voice loud enough to be heard by others, to stop their blocking manœuvres and to vote for Montini. He appealed to the curial party to consider the general good of the Church and not to dissipate the goodwill won by Pope John's pontificate. Testa, a jolly fat man, who was always speaking out of turn, should not have done it. But it helped to break the deadlock.

Later the same night another source reports that Cardinal König of Vienna met Cardinal Montini in the Galleria del Lapidorio, and found him looking sad and worried. König did his best to console him. 'That's all very well,' said Montini, 'but I still hope that I won't be elected. Sometimes the votes rise to a certain level and then stay there. I hope that will happen to me.' He sighed and added: 'For the moment I'm in darkness and cannot see anything clearly.' Next morning he had the necessary majority on the fifth ballot. The curial party – or enough of it – had been won over, perhaps with the promise that Cicognani, one of their men, would be Secretary of State. In the end they were prepared to accept Montini in order to avert the greater evil – in their eyes – of Lercaro, who might well have decided to abandon the Vatican and live in a Rome slum. No one quite knew what he would do. He had turned his archiepiscopal palace into a hostel for homeless boys. As Cardinal Lercaro knelt before the new pope to present his homage, Pope Paul said: 'That's how life is, your eminence – you should be sitting here.'

This reconstruction   which Pope Paul would have been able to read – helps to explain why *Romano Pontifici Eligendo* imposed such stringent conditions of secrecy and why it was so fierce in its rejection of pacts or deals. A pope is not free if he has to accept So-and-so as his Secretary of State. This was a point of great importance for Pope Paul. It was he who decreed that all the principal offices of the Roman Curia should lapse on the death of the pope. The events of 1963 Cardinal Testa came out saying that 'Terrible things happened'   might also explain the exclusion of the over-eighties from the conclave. It was uncharacteristic of Pope Paul gratuitously to wound the sensibilities of the old men, and yet he did hurt them by taking away the sole function to which the rank of cardinal entitled them: the right to elect the next pope. The only explanation is that he wanted to spare his successor the trouble that he had experienced.

The first thing to be said about the August conclave is that the revision of the procedure proved effective, in the sense that the conclave was short, unacrimonious, and left the cardinals feeling that they had worked well and experienced the presence of the Holy Spirit. Though the traditional canopies had been abolished (the new pope alone used to leave his canopy open above his head after his election), nothing was changed in the method of voting. On the tables were the ballot papers with the printed formula *Eligo in Summum Pontificum* ('I elect as Supreme Pontiff'). Below that on the morning of 26 August the cardinals wrote the name of their chosen candidate, and they were recommended to disguise their handwriting so that no one could recognize it. Then, having folded the paper in two, they advanced in turn towards the altar, knelt for a moment in prayer, and pronounced the oath: 'I call to witness Christ the Lord who will be my judge, that my vote is given to the one whom before God I consider should be elected.' The cardinal then placed his ballot paper on the paten and tipped it into the chalice on the altar. It is an awesome act beneath the gaze of Michelangelo's severe, chastising Christ. When everyone had voted, the ballot papers were shuffled and the three scrutineers began their work. The first took out a ballot paper, read it silently, made a note, and handed it on to the second scrutineer, who did the same; the third scrutineer read out the name, and the cardinals could make their own tally. Then the ballot papers were threaded together and prepared for burning, two ballots at a time.

It is easy enough to provide an account of the procedure. It is less easy to say what actually happened. The two undoubted facts are that a surprise candidate, Albino Luciani, was elected, and elected within a single day. The August conclave conformed to no previous pattern. Anything further than that will be a matter of informed interpretation. Nevertheless we are not completely at a loss in trying to penetrate the mystery of the conclave.

It was Pope John Paul himself who provided the first important clue. When he appeared on the balcony of St Peter's for the *Angelus* at noon on the day after his election, he began by saying:

Yesterday morning I went to the Sistine Chapel to vote peacefully. I would never have imagined what was about to take place. As soon as things became dangerous for me, two of my colleagues whispered words of encouragement. One of them said: 'Courage, if the Lord gives a burden, he also gives the strength to carry it.' And the other said: 'Don't be afraid, the whole world is praying for the new pope.' Then, when the moment came, I accepted it.

It was not difficult to identify the two colleagues. Cardinal Jan Willebrands was seated on his right, and Cardinal Antonio Ribeiro of Lisbon was on his left. But the significance of Pope John Paul's remarks is that there was a moment in the conclave when 'things began to look dangerous for me'. That presupposes a before and after. That is to say that there was first a moment when things did not look particularly dangerous, followed by a moment of great danger when he needed consolation, and then, finally, the moment of election and acceptance. Expressed in terms of ballots, that would indicate that Cardinal Luciani received a fair but by no means decisive number of votes in the first ballot, that he gained considerable momentum in the second ballot, and a sufficient majority by the third (more than 75). That would square with the remark of one of the *conclavista* who noted that the mood at lunch on the Saturday was one of relaxation and joy in the Lord, compared with the rather solemn supper of the previous evening. They could already see a pope beginning to emerge and felt that he would have a large consensus. This was a point of some importance because it meant that the conclave, instead of presenting to the watching world the spectacle of divided cardinals locked in conflict and arguing for days over the succession, would rapidly and harmoniously elect the new pope. This contributed powerfully to the feeling that the Holy Spirit was present.

It also created a feeling of euphoria which helped to release inhibitions and loosen tongues. There can be no doubt that the eventual majority was well above the mere 75 required. Cardinal Joseph Höffner of Cologne immediately despatched an enthusiastic pastoral letter to his diocese in which he said that in the final ballot, 'There was no need to count the names, because the only name read out by the scrutineers was that of Luciani.' He also revealed that there had been 'loud applause from all the cardinals' when the last ballot paper was read out. Cardinal Luciani then took his place on the chair set before the altar, and his first words were (still according to Cardinal Höffner's pastoral letter): 'God will forgive you for what you have done to me.' The idea that there was virtual unanimity at the end was supported by Vatican Radio, which has privileged status. Its commentator said that the election was 'almost by acclamation' (*'quasi un'acclamazione'*). More important was the witness of Cardinal Léon-Joseph Suenens who in interviews with *Le Soir* and *La Libre Belgique*, both Brussels newspapers, declared that the first ballot was scattered and inconclusive (it was a *vote de sondage*, a testing out of the ground), that in the second ballot there were far fewer names, that by the third the way ahead was clear, and that by the fourth there was 'an extraordinary, unexpected majority, a royal three-quarters'. Three-quarters of 111 is 84, so 'a royal three-quarters' must presumably be rather more than that. The Suenens analysis was confirmed by Cardinal Franz König who said: 'At the start opinions were very divided. One thought that the conclave was going to be long and arduous. But then there was a convergence of votes in the third ballot but especially in the fourth.' The general pattern of the conclave is clear: Cardinal Luciani's candidature moved from uncertainty to possibility and from probability to triumph.

These accounts from three European cardinals of undoubted honesty presuppose that there were four ballots. There was certainly time for four. If two took place in the morning between 9.30 and noon, then two could have taken place in the afternoon between four o'clock and 6.30 when the first puffs of what were meant to be white smoke appeared. But other sources speak of three ballots. *Civiltà Cattolica*, the semi-official Jesuit fortnightly review and adult version of *Osservatore Romano*, said in an editorial: 'Pope John Paul was elected, it seems, on the third ballot.' That cautious 'it seems' may provide a clue. Suppose that he was elected on the third ballot (i.e. that he had more than 75 votes) and that he then asked for a confirming ballot just to make sure that no one could have any juridical objection to his election. Lefebvre, it will be recalled, had said that he would reject in advance any candidate emerging from a conclave which excluded the over-eighties. There were sixteen over-eighties. A confirming vote would have dealt neatly with this problem and explain the near-unanimity of the final vote to which Cardinal Höffner referred.

But we still have not come any closer towards explaining how it was that the virtually unknown Cardinal Luciani gained so sweeping and rapid a victory. And the well-attested near-unanimity in the final ballot (whether it was the third or the fourth) meant that almost any cardinal, or group of cardinals, could let it be known without breaking the secret that he or they had contributed to Cardinal Luciani's success. The common conviction that the Holy Spirit had been at work was another way of saying that they were extremely satisfied with the outcome. Cardinal Suenens expressed this feeling most strikingly when he quoted the remark of one of the heroes of his youth, Fr Vincent Lebbe. Lebbe once emerged from an audience with Pius XI who had told him to go to China and ordain five bishops of his own choosing. Lebbe said: '*Je ne crois plus au Saint Esprit – je l'ai vu*' ('I no longer *believe* in the Holy Spirit I have *seen* him'). Suenens applied this saying to the conclave. However, our witnesses also make it clear that this remarkable convergence did not happen right from the start. Who, then, had launched the movement in favour of Cardinal Luciani? We have already seen that he was Cardinal Benelli's candidate, and that the Archbishop of Florence was far from slothful in promoting his man.

But an equally important influence was Cardinal Confalonieri. At eighty-five he was excluded from the conclave. But as Dean of the Sacred College he was not only present at the pre-conclave General Congregations but presided at them. When he appeared on RAI (Italian TV) on the night of the election, he could hardly contain his joy. The bubbling spontaneity of his answers no doubt gave away more than he intended. He was naturally asked whether the result was a surprise. He replied:

It was certainly not a surprise for me or for the other cardinals. The name of Patriarch Luciani was one that had attracted the attention of the cardinal electors in the last days of the pre-conclave period. The press missed this altogether, perhaps because it was misled by the modest and reserved attitude of the Patriarch of Venice. I have to admit that, at the start, a number of cardinals did not know him well (*a fondo*), but this could no longer be said after the various daily meetings that were held under my presidency.

This was a barely veiled confession that he had worked hard for his candidate – Luciani – and seen to it that he became better known to the electors. The fact that Luciani's name had attracted increasing attention 'in the last days of the pre-conclave period' is also important: for it was only then that the general discussion on what sort of pope the Church needed moved from Identikit portraits to actual names (and even then, not officially). But Confalonieri, veteran of four previous conclaves, was not surprised. One is surprised when the unexpected happens. The election of Luciani was expected.

But there was another factor in the election which made it less surprising for those in the know: the relationship that existed between Cardinal Luciani and Cardinal Lorscheider – and through Lorscheider with the Latin Americans generally. The Patriarch of Venice had not travelled much – this was one of the objections against him – but he had been to Brazil two years before to deal with the pastoral problems of Italians working there. Lorscheider said of that visit: 'On that occasion many people hazarded the guess that one day the Patriarch of Venice could become pope'. The esteem was mutual. On his return from Brazil, Cardinal Luciani had confided in a Venetian priest that he would be happy to see Lorscheider as pope. 'He is a man of faith and culture', he said, 'and he has a good knowledge of Italy and of Italian.' He added: 'The time has come to choose a pope from the third world.' Cardinal Evaristo Arns, like Lorscheider a Brazilian and a Franciscan, also gave a revealing interview after the conclave: 'The Patriarch of Venice was probably better known to us than to you [in Italy]. I knew him because I was made a cardinal along with him in May 1973 and he was the first of our group. The first time we met in Rome we began to talk about the poor and the third world. What he said and wrote on these questions was always reported in our press' (Interview with Domenico del Rio in *La Repubblica*, 29 August 1978). This establishes that Luciani was not the unknown figure in Latin America that he was in the 'Anglo-Saxon' world. But more directly

illuminating on the conclave was Arns' further comment:
'In the first phase (*in un primo tempo*) we would have liked
a pope from the third world. But then, thinking that he
should be an Italian, we decided to choose someone who
loved the third world.' The expression 'in the first phase'
cannot possibly refer to anything that happened within the
conclave itself, when there was no time for such discussions:
it must obviously refer to the pre-conclave period. The Latin
Americans – or most of them – had decided on their candidate in advance.

None of this means that the conclave was a foregone
conclusion. Support from Benelli, Confalonieri and the Latin
Americans was enough to launch a candidate, but not to
guarantee his success. There was still a contest, especially
in the first ballot where, all witnesses agree, the votes were
dispersed. That was only to be expected. As one cardinal
remarked: 'In the first ballot I will vote for somebody that I
want – after that I will let the Holy Spirit guide me.' But
that is about as far as it is possible to go relying on comments made by those who were directly involved in the
conclave.

One author, Fr F. X. Murphy, has however gone much
further and provided a detailed breakdown of the voting.
The distinguished Redemptorist knows the Vatican well and
was commonly held to be the principal author of *Letters from
Vatican City* and three subsequent volumes on the Council.
They remain the best account in English of Vatican II. A
conclave, though, is by definition a much more elusive event
than a Council, and indiscretions are harder to come by.
Fr Murphy did not clearly indicate his sources. He hinted
at them in the following sentence: 'The new pope's cheerful
indiscretion [i.e. on the 'danger' he underwent] was sufficient to relax the fine Italian consciences of a few cardinals
who seemed anxious to let the world know how they had
chosen the Church's latest *Pontifex Maximus*' (*Newsweek*,
11 September 1978). Of course cardinals who are not Italian
can possess a 'fine Italian conscience', whatever that is, but
the inference is that it was Italian cardinals who talked if

anyone talked. According to these sources, the ballots in the conclave went as follows:

1st ballot	2nd ballot	3rd ballot
Siri 25	Luciani 56	Luciani 'over 90'
Luciani 23	Pignedoli 15	Pignedoli 17
Pignedoli 18	Lorscheider 12	Lorscheider
Baggio 9	Baggio 10	'at least 1'
König 8	Felici 8	
Bertoli 5 or 6	Cordeiro 4	
Pironio 4	plus 6 single	
Felici 2	votes	
Lorscheider 2		
plus 24 single		
votes		

This account agrees to some extent with what has already been said, but it has a number of odd features which provide material for further reflection.

The agreements first. The wide scatter of votes cast in the first ballot is confirmed (and if the 24 single votes of unnamed candidates are added to the 9 named candidates, then no less than 33 cardinals were thought worth a vote by their peers – surely a record). The 'danger' is evident from the second ballot, for at that point Cardinal Luciani has a simple majority of 56 as against a dispersed 55, and that is not a losing position. Election is secured at the third ballot, but a fourth confirming ballot is not excluded by these figures (Cardinal Höffner had said that the name of Luciani was the only one read out).

Now for the oddities. The first is that Cardinal Siri, who is in the lead in the first ballot, disappears altogether from the second. Whoever voted for him must have concluded that he had already 'peaked', and that, despite his lead, there was no point in continuing to vote for him. What is remarkable is that this conclusion was reached unanimously and at a time when there was no pause for discussion: the second ballot followed immediately on the first. The candidature of Siri, a self-confessed conservative, can only have been put forward by the Roman Curia (or the most organized group within it). Having noted that most of the cardinals had said that they wanted a 'pastoral' pope, it seemed to them that the non-curial Italian who best suited their book was Siri. His warning against 'irrational suggestions' now makes more sense: he was opposed to the election of a third world pope on a great wave of uncritical enthusiasm. Again, it was only a coherent group like the curial cardinals with a thought-out strategy who could – without discussion – have abandoned their original candidate. Most of them must have switched to Luciani in the second ballot. But why did this happen? The curial mistrust of Pignedoli was no secret. He was said to be naïve and light-weight intellectually. Ossobuco's remarks reflected their views accurately. Given, therefore, the outcome of the first ballot, and determined to stop Pignedoli, they immediately switched to Luciani whom they would not have chosen but whom they had nothing against. He might even be more manageable. This was confirmed by their enthusiasm for the eventual result. Luciani was not their candidate but he rapidly became their candidate. At this point everything was working in his favour, though in the second ballot one can see a doomed attempt to build up a third world candidate (Lorscheider's 12 and Cordeiro's 4) and two fall-back curial candidates (Baggio's 10 and Felici's 8).

The oddest feature of the Murphy figures is the role assigned to Pignedoli in the third ballot. That Luciani should have had 'over 90' is possible and even probable (Cardinal Suenens' 'royal three-quarters'): but that the hard-core, recalcitrant opposition to him should have come from Pignedoli supporters seems implausible. In effect, a vote for Pignedoli would have been 'a vote for Pope Paul but with a smile'; and once Luciani had emerged from obscurity, that was exactly what a vote for him signified. So why should Pignedoli supporters have held out against him when they knew that theirs was a lost cause? It would make no sense at all. There is, however, an alternative

explanation: that the votes for Pignedoli did not come from
true Pignedoli supporters (who had already switched) but
from die-hard opponents of Luciani who, observing the
result of the second ballot, found Pignedoli the only possible
candidate, apart from Luciani, who still had the faintest
chance of success, and so gave Pignedoli their 'protest' vote.
The whole meaning of the conclave depends on the identifi-
cation of this group of 'dissidents'. The Murphy account
suggests without asserting that they were Pignedoli men.
Another version, given by Giancarlo Zizola, suggests on
the contrary that they were unyielding conservatives to
whom even the moderate Luciani seemed dangerously progressive. Zizola's evidence is the statement made by the
Argentinian Cardinal Juan Carlos Aramburu, a noted conservative, who alone of all the cardinals admitted that he
had not voted for Luciani (*Il Giorno*, 29 August 1978).
Zizola also explains that the 'dissidents' returned empty
ballot papers – which would fit in with Cardinal Höffner's
remarks about no other names being heard. I accept the
Zizola interpretation, and conclude that Cardinal Luciani
was elected by a grand and spontaneous coalition of third
world cardinals, moderates, progressives, and flexible conservatives, and that the irreducible opposition was small
and impenitently right-wing.

In the last two paragraphs I have assumed, as a hypoth-
esis, the general validity of the Murphy figures. In the
nature of the case they can be neither denied nor confirmed.
But Fr Murphy is too good a Vaticanologist not to know
that the supposed release of secret information in Rome
does not happen without some hidden intent. One does not
have to be a student of Machiavelli, though it may help,
to realize that 'fine Italian consciences' are stretched only
for a purpose. And his scenario is intended to make two
things perfectly clear: first, that the Roman Curia played
an important role in the conclave, and secondly, that
Cardinal Pignedoli was defeated and discredited. The
obvious conclusion is that his sources were to be found
somewhere in the Roman Curia. Whether they are now

excommunicated or not is a question they can discuss with their confessors. But this is only one of the sub-mysteries locked within the general mystery of the conclave. There is an illuminating saying which asserts that in Rome everything is a mystery, and nothing is in the end a secret.

The one firm certainty was that we had a pope and that his name was Albino Luciani. It remained to tell the world. At 6.25 p.m., Cardinal Pironio, no doubt relieved to be no longer the unofficial favourite of the third world and happy to be the chief stove-tender, packed the ballot papers into the stove, added the entire stock of 'chemical sticks' marked *bianco*, and struck a match. He cannot have known the uncertain nature of his smoke-signals. Outside in St Peter's Square, the modest crowd, which was expecting more black smoke on this first day of the conclave, saw what appeared to be black smoke and prepared to go home. At 6.30, however, there were four more distinct puffs of smoke, of a somewhat indeterminate grey, but it was difficult to judge against the evening sky, which was turning a pearly white. Then there was a more continuous stream of smoke, but experienced judges said it was grey and therefore intended to be black. It was only at 7.15 that a loud-speaker of Vatican Radio announced that the smoke was definitely white. The suspense could not have been greater, and there was a hint of farce. One sympathized with the Italian designer who had exhibited an electric stove that could, on the push of a button, produce up to fifty colours. At 7.18 Cardinal Pericle Felici resolved all doubts by appearing on the balcony of St Peter's and saying, in the traditional manner: '*Annuncio vobis gaudium magnum: habemus papam, Albinum Luciani, qui sibi imposuit nomen Ioannem Paulum primum*'.

Scattered cheers greeted the news that 'we had a pope'. Next morning at breakfast Felici said to an American cardinal that this was for him and the crowd the supreme moment: without a pope, the Church felt bereft, orphaned, and who was pope was of less significance. But the real interest of the announcement lay elsewhere. When he gave the name *Albinum* there was merely polite applause. In 1963 it was enough for the name Giovanni Battista to be pronounced for the crowd to chant 'Montini, Montini'. But this time people looked at each other and wondered who Albino was. Albino who? 'Luciani', said Felici, savouring the moment, but few were much wiser. At least he sounded Italian. It is only fair to add that in the holiday month of August the crowd was made up of tourists rather than knowledgeable Romans. Felici went on: 'Who has chosen the name John Paul I.' (The first edition of *Osservatore Romano*, out two hours later, contained a dreadful howler: '*Qui sibi nominem imposuit* . . .' it said in bold type. The edition was withdrawn and became a collector's item.) John Paul was puzzling at first, and rather cumbersome in Italian: it was soon abbreviated to Gianpaolo. But one got the general idea: it was a tribute to both his predecessors, John who had ordained him bishop in 1958, and Paul who had made him a cardinal in 1973.

But there was no denying the surprise at the speed of the conclave and astonishment at its outcome. Cardinals, pressed for instant comment, evoked the Holy Spirit. Cardinal Terence J. Cooke of New York was asked: 'Were you shocked by the result?' He replied: 'Surprised would be a nicer word: the Holy Spirit brought us together in a wonderful, spiritual way.' Cardinal Silvio Oddi said that it had been 'like an inspiration'. Cardinal Benelli said: 'The Holy Spirit has given us a pope in record time. He enabled us to grasp something that some had doubted: the unity of the Church.' Cardinal Stefan Wyszinski had a slightly different theory: he reminded everyone that on the day of the conclave, over a million pilgrims had been praying at the shrine of Our Lady of Czestochowa in Poland, and that no doubt had something to do with the result. It was left to Cardinal Basil Hume to make the definitive comment the next day: 'Seldom have I had such an experience of the presence of God . . . I am not one for whom the dictates of the Holy Spirit are self-evident. I'm slightly hard-boiled on that . . . But for me he was God's candidate.'

Meanwhile the new pope was telephoning Mgr Matteo

Ducoli, Bishop of his own diocese of Belluno, to send greetings to his brother Edoardo, his sister Nina, his nephews,
nieces and friends. 'Holy Father,' asked the astonished
bishop, 'can I tell people that I spoke to you on the telephone?' 'Of course you can,' said Pope John Paul, 'that is
why I called you.' The Bishop told the people of Belluno
the next day. Pope John Paul stayed in his 'cell' on the
night of his election rather than move into the papal apartments. He had to work throughout the night on his address
to the cardinals the next morning. He had asked them to
stay on in the conclave area for another night. This speech
was the first act of his pontificate. It belongs to a later
chapter.

7

Albino Who?

*So the young Luciani went to two local seminaries, kicked
footballs around on arid playgrounds, ate an unbalanced
diet, learned a didactic rather than a questioning theology,
was given the answers before he was allowed to put the
questions.*

Patrick O'Donovan, *The Observer*,
3 September 1978

That one of Pope John Paul's first acts should have been
to ring the local bishop and get in touch with his brother,
Edoardo, was entirely typical: he was loyal to his family
and his region. But Edoardo was rather put out by all the
fuss. He still lives in the grey two-storey family house in
Canale d'Agordo (its name was changed from Forno di
Canale in 1964), a village of 1500 inhabitants. According
to the sign which greets the visitor when he arrives, it stands
976 metres above sea-level. Edoardo has risen to be Chair-
man of the Chamber of Commerce of Belluno, is universally
known as 'maestro Berto', and found his new role as pope's
brother rather trying. He went along to the special Mass of
thanksgiving in the afternoon of Monday 28 August, and
was ushered into the front row so that photographers could
get a better picture. He said afterwards: 'It's difficult to be
pope – but it's even more difficult to be the pope's brother.
I can't get any work done with all these journalists pestering
me from morning till night. I would like to send them all
to the devil, but what would my brother the pope say? He's
landed me in a fine mess' (reported by Marco Nozza in *Il
Giorno*, 29 August 1978). Their eighty-year-old aunt, in her
black veil, said simply: 'Poor Don Albino'. Toni Cagnata,

the communist mayor of Canale d'Agordo, who had not been seen in the church for over twenty years, turned up that afternoon full of civic pride, put out all the flags, and later organized coaches to take the citizens to the inauguration. The whole episode had the flavour of Don Camillo. It was so homely, so very Italian.

But life was not easy for Albino's parents, Giovanni and Bortola (née Toncon), when he was born on 17 October 1912. Giovanni had been widowed and there were two daughters from his previous marriage. After Albino came Edoardo and a daughter, Nina. Bortola was an educated woman who wrote letters for illiterates, but to earn money she had to go into domestic service and at one time worked for a Jewish family – a fact that her son remembered when pope. Though her husband Giovanni later found work in the glass works at Murano, at this time he had to cross the mountains to Germany or Switzerland where he took seasonal jobs as a bricklayer or electrician. He would leave in the spring and return as winter set in. His eldest son was baptized Albino in memory of one of his workmates who was killed in a blast-furnace accident in Germany. The men of Belluno still have to emigrate to find work. In Germany Giovanni picked up socialist ideas. This led to a family quarrel that Luciani did not forget. One day his mother, who was extremely pious, came home from Mass in a state of some agitation: she had seen her husband's name on the socialist list for the municipal elections. At that date in Italy, to be a socialist was to be a *mangeur de curés*, but Bertola worked on her husband so that he had no objection when Albino wanted to enter the seminary; and his first act on returning from abroad was always to visit his eldest son. If he wanted grandchildren, he could count on his other son, Edoardo, who eventually had eleven children, and his daughter, Nina, who married a bricklayer and more modestly had two children. The result was that the Luciani are today a far-flung family, and cousins have been discovered in odd corners of the world: there is Silvio Luciani, who lives in a caravan at Marysville, Michigan, and Gino

Scardanzu, a carpenter, who lives in Edmonton, Canada. There is another cousin in Warrington, England. Albino Luciani was the first pope to have had a working-class background. There had been sons of peasants before him, but no sons of workers in the post-Marx sense. When later on in Venice he sold precious church objects, and encouraged his priests to do the same, he said, remembering St Ambrose, 'the poor are the real treasures of the Church' this was no mere figure of speech. It reflected his experience of poverty in childhood.

He came to know the Veneto region well. As bishop he tramped all over his diocese and turned up in remote mountain villages that could not remember having seen a bishop before. He was known as 'the bishop in the big boots'. The Veneto is a region of poverty, piety and contrasts: it is icily cold in winter and swelteringly hot in summer. The people are shrewd, hard-working, hospitable. They give the visitor the traditional dishes – *risotto* and *risi-bisi* (rice and peas) and *polenta* (made from maize flour). They are liberal with wine. Even those who have never been to Veneto can form some idea of its landscape from the paintings of Giorgione. One of his most famous paintings is in the cathedral of Castelfranco Veneto, not far from Luciani's first diocese of Vittoria Veneto: the Madonna and child are framed by the soaring blue peaks of the Dolomites which rise above the village of Canale d'Agordo; at the side stand peasants in a lush meadow beneath a medieval castle.

One of the wrenching things about becoming pope is that one is unlikely ever to return to the place where one was born. Yet the last three popes, all from northern provinces, have been greatly attached to their place of birth. Pope John came from Bergamo, a fact he let no one forget, and he had written the life of Radini, Bishop of Bergamo, in his youth. Pope Paul came from Brescia, and mentioned it nostalgically in his will. Pope John Paul had spent most of his life in and around the Veneto. But this keen sense of place does not lead to provincialism. As Paul Johnson said of Pope John: 'Roncalli was by instinct a regionalist; and this provided the basis for his subsequent convictions as an internationalist (*Pope John XXIII*, Hutchinson, London, 1975, p. 6). The same paradox also applied to Pope John Paul I: if the sense of national identity is weak in Italy, the feeling for loyalties on a human scale is strong, and this makes Italians find nationalism repugnant and inclined to regard all men, in their splendid diversity, as brothers.

As was the custom, Albino Luciani embarked on the long road to the priesthood by going to the minor seminary at Feltre. The English-speaking world – helped by scarifying images in Italian neo-realist films – has had a low view of minor seminaries in which small boys were removed from their parents at an early age, were dressed in cassocks as mini-priests, and walked out two by two in long crocodiles. Some would be scarred for life by the experience. Luciani was saved from narrowness by reading widely and using his imagination. In his book *Illustrissimi* he describes how he first read Dickens' *Christmas Carol* curled up in a corner, and somehow a link was established in his mind between poverty in Victorian England and the poverty he knew in Belluno. To be a priest was his way of serving the poor. Mussolini was in power, and there was no form of political activity open to a Catholic. Nor could he have done much in journalism at that date – he had always confessed, as though it were a guilty secret, that if he had not been a priest he would have been a journalist, of the crusading, not the gossipy, type.

So he moved on to the major seminary, the Gregorian of Belluno, 45 kilometres from Canale d'Agordo, as a form of 'inner emigration'. One of his professors there was Alfredo (later Cardinal) Ottaviani who could be counted on to provide manual-theology in all its intransigent rigour. The official biography chastely makes no mention of his military service, but a photograph survives to prove that the young Luciani looked dashing in military uniform and sported a fine moustache (as did Roncalli in the same circumstances). He was ordained priest on 7 July 1935. His seminary professors thought him promising enough to be sent to the Gregorian University in Rome for higher studies. The 'Greg' has produced so many bishops, cardinals and popes over the years – Pope John was the odd man out among the popes of this century – that the university authorities have lost count. At the Gregorian University, gushed the official biography, 'he gained his doctorate in theology with a brilliant thesis on Rosmini'. That is a misleading statement in two respects: he did not complete his thesis until after the war and, according to one good judge who has read it, 'the thesis was a mere rehash of out-worn apologetic arguments'. The director of the thesis was Fr Charles Boyer S.J., a pioneer ecumenist who is still alive at the age of 93. He was glad to have taught a future pope, but could remember nothing whatever about him: so many generations and so many theses have passed by. Luciani chose as his subject: 'The Problem of the Origin of the Soul in Rosmini'. But the fact that he was drawn to Rosmini at all is interesting. Rosmini was still vaguely suspect – he had been the victim of Jesuit intrigues in the mid-nineteenth century, but his complete works existed in the Belluno seminary: they had been presented by Pope Gregory XVI who also came from Belluno and had been Rosmini's patron. Whatever Luciani may have thought of Rosmini's speculative theology, he was later to show that he had the highest opinion of *The Five Wounds of the Church*, one of the great reforming influences on Italian catholicism.

After his Roman studies he returned to his own parish of Canale d'Agordo where he was appointed curate or assistant priest, the humblest clerical status known in the Church. He also taught religion in the local Technical Institute of Mining; its pupils almost invariably had to go to Belgium to find work. After a brief stint in the parish, he became vice-rector of the Seminary of Belluno in the autumn of 1937, and spent the next ten years turning his hand to everything, from dogmatic theology to scripture, morals, patristics, the history of art, canon law, not forgetting sacred eloquence. He became, in other words, a 'generalist' rather than a specialist, and was not the first to have learned theology by having to teach it to others. It can be the worst of methods; it can be the best. The present parish priest of Canale d'Agordo, Don Rinaldo Andrich, was one of his students. He recalled that 'Don Albino always managed to make the most difficult questions interesting'. While still teaching in the seminary, he became vicar general to Gerolamo Bordignon, Bishop of Belluno (later transferred to Padua) and a friend of Pope John. During the war Bordignon, a tough, bearded Capuchin, had once appealed to the local German commander to save a group of resistance fighters and hostages from execution. His appeal failed, and he offered his own life instead. In vain. The bodies were left dangling on the trees of Belluno for days.

After the war and a spell in a sanatorium – he had been threatened by tuberculosis as a boy – Luciani began to take on wider responsibilities. He was secretary of the inter-diocesan Synod of Feltre and Belluno in 1947. His interest in the practical, communicable aspect of theology opened naturally into catechetics. In 1949 he was made responsible for catechetics in preparation for the Eucharistic Congress of the diocese of Belluno that year. He recorded the substance of his experience in a book, *Catechesi in Bricole (Catechesis in easy stages* or *Crumbs from the Catechism)*. Catechetics is not the branch of theology that is most highly regarded by professional theologians – and some would deny that it belongs to theology at all. But it has ceased to mean the question-and-answer method of teaching children and become the study of how to embody Christian values in life. It was characteristic of Luciani that he should have been concerned not with theology as an abstract study but with its implementation in everyday life. In a later interview (1969) with Alberto Papuzzi he said that for him the central religious problem was 'the gap between a purely formal and nominal Christianity, based merely on ideas, and an existential Christianity that finds expression in life'. No doubt this perception of the problem matured gradually. But his concern that faith should move, to use Newman's phrase, 'from notional to real assent', had been one of the constants of his pastoral work.

By 1958 Don Luciani was 46. His mother had died in 1948 and his father in 1952. The long pontificate of Pius XII had come to an end – its last years characterized by a certain weariness and mistrust of theologians – and Pope John XXIII had succeeded him. In the celebrated phrase, he 'opened the windows of the Vatican' (and, say his critics, let the winds of the world howl through). One of his first acts was to name Albino Luciani Bishop of Vittoria Veneto and to insist on ordaining him bishop himself, in St Peter's on 27 December 1958. In the photograph taken on that occasion one sees the massive back of Pope John and the slim, youthful-looking, not yet bespectacled figure of Luciani. His appointment had come in record time: the see had been vacant for only fifteen days. It came about because Pope John had summoned his friend Bishop Bordignon to dinner one night and asked him for suggestions. Bordignon proposed the name of Luciani, and Pope John accepted his judgement. The clerical old-boy-network had operated. Luciani had in fact already met Pope John during a train journey. But as Luciani explained afterwards: 'He couldn't possibly have remembered who I was, because he did all the talking'. Perhaps Roncalli was more perceptive than he thought.

He was a bishop, said witnesses at the time, 'in the Pope John mould'. He was always available to his priests, and regularly had three priests or seminarians to dinner in the evening. He consulted before deciding. He was seen everywhere in his rugged mountain diocese. He was a friend of Cardinal Giacomo Lercaro, who shared his judgement that the Church should be above all the Church of the poor. A scandal in the diocese gave him an opportunity to illustrate this practically. Two priests had squandered parish funds and were in debt for hundreds of millions of *lire*. Bishop Luciani did not believe that they should be exempted from a civil action, and gathered the four hundred priests of the diocese to explain why: clerical exemption could never be a cover for injustice. He then paid their debts from the proceeds of the sale of ecclesiastical treasures. In all this could be seen the influence of Rosmini who had finally published his great work, *The Five Wounds of the Church*, in 1848, judging that the new pope, Pio Nono, would not mind him 'speaking frankly about the ills of the Church'. The title was suggested by a speech of Pope Innocent IV to the Council of Lyons, in which he had compared the Church to Christ on the cross with his five wounds. For Rosmini the five wounds were: the separation of the people from the clergy in worship; the defective education of priests; disunity among bishops; the nomination of bishops by the secular power; and the Church's enslavement to wealth.

Meanwhile Pope John had unexpectedly announced the summoning of Vatican Council II: in his mind it was to be a way of extending to the whole Church the best thinking of parts of the Church. To some extent Luciani had already anticipated the Council in his diocese. But it was to be a time of decisive importance for him. For four long sessions, annually from 1962 to 1965, he had a chance to read and study. Yet he never spoke in the Council, though he did submit written interventions on Our Lady and on collegiality. They did not attract much attention. After all, what is one bishop among 2,200? By his own account, he stayed in the background during the Council, kept out of the intrigues of his fellow Italian bishops, and spent the evenings studying the draft texts. He had a room in the Roman minor seminary, and from his window he could see Pope John saying his breviary on the terrace of the Torre di San Giovanni. He was rather isolated, though he made contacts with Belgian theologians (reported Cardinal Suenens) and with the Germans, whose language he knew best. For him, the Council was a matter of 'conversion and going back to school'. It gave him an unrivalled opportunity to renew his theological thinking. His greatest difficulty with the Council, he freely admitted, was caused by its declaration *On Religious Freedom*. He had been taught by Cardinal Ottaviani in the Belluno seminary that 'error had no rights' and that, consequently, the toleration of Protestants was impossible where Catholics were in a majority. This illiberal doctrine – traceable to Pio Nono and his *Syllabus of Errors* – evidently cut at the root of ecumenism. It was challenged at the Council especially by American bishops and their *peritus*, John Courtney Murray. Luciani pondered the matter and changed his mind. He said later: 'I studied the question in depth, and reached the conclusion that we had been wholly wrong.' But he was less happy with the American bishops on another question. The Council had prepared a strong statement on the armaments race. It had denounced the 'balance of terror' as an unreliable method of maintaining peace and went on: 'While extravagant sums are being spent on the furnishing of ever new weapons, an adequate remedy cannot be provided for the many miseries afflicting the whole modern world' (*The Church in the World of Today*, 81). Luciani said: 'No doubt Cardinal Spellman saw in this an attack on U.S. policy, but today the Church cannot refuse to commit itself on this question.'

Back in his diocese of Vittoria Veneto, he continued to live in the Castle of San Martino, on the hill of Ceneda, where his predecessors had been the count-bishops of Ottone and later the prince-bishops of great Venetian families. But, as he told Zizola in 1969, his whole aim had been to transform the Church from a defensive fortress into a missionary community. The Council had confirmed the policies he had already begun to adopt in Vittoria Veneto. He stated his priorities clearly: liturgical reform; the education of the clergy – he recommended them to read the theological reviews rather than their old manuals – and the need for poverty in the Church. Instead of the conventional form of the pastoral letter, he began to write once a week to his priests, to share his thoughts and keep the programme before them. It was straight out of Rosmini. He was also interested in another Rosmini thesis: that bishops should be directly elected by clergy and people. He did not think that it could work out in practice, because of the local jealousies and rivalries that would be aroused. But he accepted the principle of participation, and suggested that the local community should propose a list of several names to the pope.

Many bishops, who imagine that they have been parachuted down on their dioceses by the Holy Spirit, would not have been prepared even to entertain the idea.

The same openness to new ideas – or to rediscovered old ones – could be seen in the way he trusted his pastoral council and senate of priests. They were made up of elected, not nominated, members, and Bishop Luciani accepted their decisions even when they went against him. He disagreed, for instance, when they wanted to close down one of the junior seminaries, but he let them have their way. 'And I haven't regretted it,' he added. But he did not think of the seminary as a separated hot-house, sent the seminarians to state schools, and welcomed the adult vocations that started to flow in Vittoria Veneto as 'a sign of the times'. Priests were encouraged to study in other dioceses. To create a link with the third world, the diocese adopted a parish in Burundi. He took the same positive approach to the more general problem of 'confusion' in the post-conciliar Church, from which Vittoria Veneto was not exempt. His attitude was summed up in a conversation with Zizola: 'The remedy is to proclaim the truth but in a positive way, stressing the essential, expressing it in a way that will make sense for contemporary people, and remaining in touch with modern culture. There is usually a grain of truth and goodness even in false opinions.' He was echoing, and no doubt knew it, the words of Pope John in his opening speech to the Council when he rounded on the 'prophets of doom' and insisted on a positive, non-judgemental approach to the modern world. Dialogue becomes impossible if one party starts off with a condemnation of the other.

Luciani's attitude to political questions was more complex. He thought that a bishop should be above all a 'religious' figure. 'Can you see me manipulating votes or managing affairs?', he asked Zizola rhetorically, 'I'm not that sort of chap. I leave financial questions to others, to experts. A bishop has other things to do, he has the Gospel . . . .' Luciani had seen public opinion change on the role of the clergy in politics, and he told Alberto Papuzzi why he was not altogether happy with the change: 'People used to say that the hierarchy should steer clear of politics; now they are beginning to demand that priests should have the right to commit themselves – just like any other man and take positions of responsibility in political parties. This does not seem to me to square with the logic of the Council. The priest is – normally – a man for all: he cannot be the man of a party or a faction. Exceptions are always possible: I am thinking of Don Sturzo and Ignatius Seipel. But we have to beware of deceiving ourselves: in time politics tends to devour those who go in for it.' He strongly approved when Cardinal Urbani, his predecessor as Patriarch of Venice, condemned the 'civic committees' of Luigi Gedda, who had tried to turn Catholic Action into an arm of the Christian Democratic Party and an ally of the Neo-Fascists. Through the 'civic committees' (which Pius XI had said were 'the apple of his eye'), the hierarchy had been able to keep a tight rein on the political activities of Catholics. By loosening this link, they were withdrawing to more neutral ground. On the other hand, Luciani did not make the Italian experience the norm for the rest of the world. Alberto Papuzzi asked him what he thought of Camilo Torres, the Colombian priest turned revolutionary. He pondered the question for some time and then said, sadly, that 'in Brazil and Colombia it was true that a few families had everything while many others went hungry'. Then he saw his visitor out.

By 1969 Luciani had been Bishop of Vittoria Veneto for eleven years. Within the Italian Conference of Bishops (CEI) he was by now well-known as a member of its doctrinal commission. Cardinal Urbani, who had succeeded Pope John as Patriarch of Venice, died unexpectedly on 17 September 1969. The search for a successor proved arduous and controversial. At first the name of Luciani was mentioned as a local candidate from the Veneto. But he was known to be reluctant to move, and so in a second phase there was talk of a 'Vatican' solution which would have brought to Venice Cardinal Antonio Samorè, a former papal diplomat and now Vatican archivist, or Mgr Franco Costa, the general assistant of Catholic Action. But then a group of a hundred Venetian laity wrote to Pope Paul to deplore the way in which the local church was completely excluded from the arcane process of finding a new Patriarch. They claimed that 'all the members of the church should take part in the choice of a bishop'. It was another echo of Rosmini. Pope Paul's answer was to consult widely, though in secret, and the result of the consultations was that once more the name of Luciani topped the list. He was appointed Patriarch of Venice on 15 December 1969.

8

Patriarch of Venice

> *Rome . . . has never maintained an easy hold over Venice.*
> *'Veneziani, poi Cristiani', is how her people used to de-*
> *scribe themselves – Venetians first, Christians afterwards.*
> James Morris, *Venice*, Faber and Faber,
> 1960, pp. 94–95

Before leaving for Venice, there was one last act to be accomplished in Vittoria Veneto. The people of the diocese clubbed together to make Luciani a donation of a million *lire*. He returned it, said it should be devoted to their own charities, and explained: 'I came to you owning nothing, and I want to leave you owning nothing.'

On 8 February 1970 Don Luciani took possession of his new diocese of Venice. He seemed a little overawed by the welcome he received. He was greeted fulsomely by the mayor, Favaretto Fisca, on the jetty of St Mark's Square. His reply was so characteristic that it is worth giving almost in full:

I am a child of the mountains who knew Venice only in imagination and as though in a dream. I thought to myself: in Venice the canals are alive with gondolas, and the gondolas are moored along them just as naturally as we tether beasts to a tree. There, among the many houses and churches, rose a tower, so meek and gentlemanly that when it decided to fall down, it took care not to hurt anyone . . . . As student and professor I came to know Venice through books. A Venice first of all built on piles in the lagoon, then much threatened, then a royal city, then the powerful Serenissima, and finally declining into a provincial capital: but all the time a unique city that could attract the admiration and the attention of the world and draw visitors to it from everywhere.

As Bishop of Vittoria Veneto I came to know it through the workers who every day 'migrated' from the diocese down to Mestre and Marghera: this was the 'other' Venice, with few monuments but so many factories, houses, spiritual problems, souls. And it is to this many-faceted city that Providence now sends me.

Signor mayor, the first Venetian coins, minted as long ago as AD 850, had the motto, 'Christ, save Venice'. I make this my own with all my heart and turn it into a prayer: 'Christ, bless Venice'.

The former professor of sacred rhetoric had struck just the right chord: he was the country boy come to town, but he knew the history of Venice and knew, too, that Venice, with its crumbling palaces and pockets of poverty, its international festivals and endless tourists, its mainland industries, its four hundred thousand inhabitants, would be an entirely different proposition from rural Veneto. Every-one was struck by his directness, simplicity and humour.

The homily pronounced the same day in a crowded St Mark's confirmed these first impressions. He referred, inevi-tably, to the two predecessors who had become popes in this century. He quoted Giuseppe Sarto (later Pope St Pius X) who had said in his inaugural sermon: 'Though I have never seen you before, I already carry you in my heart: you are my family and will remain in my love.' Luciani made these words his own: his awesome mission was towards the flock as a whole and every individual in it – and using the text of Ezekiel 34 he admitted that God found this attitude easier than bishops did. He quoted Angelo Roncalli (later Pope John XXIII), who had said when he ordained him bishop eleven years before: 'You have come to the episcopacy from teaching theology. That is an excellent thing. But it is not learning, not exquisite and abstruse language that make a good pastor, but rather complete availability to God and to men.' However, he drew no anti-intellectual conclusions from this remark and made a plea for an adult, critical faith, that was courageous in this tradition-minded city:

> Today science has developed tremendously and purified our knowledge from a thousand defects and *naïvetés* of the past; our religious knowledge, likewise, has to be cleansed of certain *naïvetés* which science contradicts and which were not, anyway, part of the authentic Christian revelation. The language and intellectual attitudes of men today have changed: and we should have the courage to change our style, offering the truth in fresh language, adapted to the new attitudes. There is today a tendency to think that religious life consists merely in worship and a few moral acts. We must, rather, make room in our whole being for the truth, and let it become the centre of our thinking so that it can direct our entire life.

He concluded his homily:

> 'You are all brothers', says the Lord. And Patriarch Roncalli liked to say: 'I am your brother Joseph.' The glory of the diocese of Venice will not be based on its magnificent churches or its splendid past, but on the efforts we make to realize fraternal union among ourselves.

The liturgy in St Mark's provided a fitting context for this homily. It was concelebrated with over a hundred priests of the diocese, and the bidding prayers or 'prayer of the faithful' were led by a young woman, a nun, and two young men. At the end of Mass, the boys of the Capella Marciana – the choir school of the Cathedral – who were scattered four by four among the congregation, sang a *Te Deum* in harmony with the male voices in the organ loft. Organs and bells pealed out. It was another Venice festival (*Il Gazzettino*, Venice, 9 February 1970).

But festivals do not last for ever, even in Venice, and the

forty-fifth Patriarch settled down to the day-to-day work of his diocese. On the day after his welcome, he visited the seminary, the women's prison of Giudecca, the male prison of Santa Maria Maggiore, and finally celebrated Mass in the church of San Simeone. He lived on the fifth floor of the patriarchal palace, a relatively modest building next to St Mark's, which gives on to the Piazzetta dei Leoncini (rather unsuccessfully rebaptized Piazza Giovanni XXIII). His oval table was a jumble of books and papers. There was a sofa and two armchairs with ochre covers, and a Byzantine icon of Our Lady that Pope John had given him. In the corner were fragments of bones – relics of the first Patriarch, Laurentius Iustiniani. The reception room was an anonymous place with red chairs and a big table for meetings. None of the pictures was particularly interesting. One of the Sisters of the Child Jesus who looked after him explained this: 'He always said that the best pictures of Venice were those one saw through the window.' The tiny chapel had room only for two kneelers. On the door of his chapel was his coat of arms: symbolic mountains of Agordo with three stars (faith, hope and charity) and the lion of St Mark, all on an azure background. His motto, *Humilitas*, was borrowed from St Charles Borromeo, canonized as 'the model of a bishop according to the Council of Trent'. According to the Sisters, he rarely watched television except for the news, and was in bed at nine o'clock and up at five in the morning. On his own admission, he ate 'like a canary' and was content in the evening with coffee and a brioche. But when he had guests he saw to it that they were well entertained. After one dinner at the palace given for the Anglican/Roman Catholic International Commission, Mgr Philippe Delhaye of Louvain joked: 'We must put off the day of reunion for as long as possible if it enables us to have meals like that.'

The evidence from Venice was that the Patriarch was more at home with children, fishermen and workers than in gilded salons, and in any case someone who went to bed at nine o'clock was unlikely to have much social life. At the annual Mass on the feast of St Peter in San Pietro in Castello, the fishermen would bring up a basket of fish at the offertory. Gondoliers hailed him as 'sior patriarca'. His sermons were full of comparisons that were sometimes homely, sometimes baroque. 'Think of me', he told the working-class parish of San Lorenzo a Mestre, 'as God's postman. Here's a letter for you, I will say. Read it, and let your answer be given in the way you lead your lives.' The motto, *Humilitas*, evidently meant something real. One feature of humility is that one does not take oneself too seriously. In Luciani's case this took the form of going through the streets of Venice incognito, dressed as a simple priest, his pectoral cross and skull cap tucked into his briefcase. He once dropped in on a conference on ecology – Venice is a city of conferences – and began to talk with one of the foreign participants. They still had plenty to say to each other when the time came for Luciani to go. He invited the ecologist to come and see him at home. 'Where do you live?' asked the ecologist. 'Just next door to San Marco.' 'Do you mean the Patriarch's palace?' 'Yes.' 'And who do I ask for?' 'Ask for the Patriarch.'

He also used his relative anonymity to fox the police. He went to Trent for the funeral of Auxiliary Bishop Ranzi, and was driven by his secretary in a grey Flavia belonging to the diocese. As they left the motorway, they saw a troop of *carabinieri* and police evidently waiting to escort them into Trent. 'Drive straight ahead,' said Luciani, 'and let's see if we can give them the slip.' The *carabinieri* paid no attention to the two very ordinary priests in their battered car. Things were a little more difficult when they arrived in Trent and were not at first recognized because the local clergy had been expecting a full escort of motor-cycled *carabinieri*.

Luciani's holidays – never longer than a week – were always spent in the convent of the Servants of Mary at Pietralba in the mountains. But for lunch he would go down to a *trattoria* in the town and enjoy his conversation with the locals, followed by a decorous game of bowls. A gregarious man, he never felt tempted to be a hermit. In his book, *Illustrissimi*, he used a letter to the anti-clerical Roman poet Giuseppe Giocchino Belli (on whom Anthony Burgess wrote a novel) to sing the praises of conversation: 'Am I downcast? The sympathy of those I am talking with consoles me. Do I feel lonely? Conversation puts an end to solitude. If it is a familiar conversation, I am happy to be admitted into intimacy with someone else; if it is an important conversation, I feel honoured at being treated as an intelligent person' (English editions will be published by William Collins, London, and Little, Brown, New York, 1978). It is difficult to convey the quality of 'simplicity' in cold print, and the anecdotes sometimes edge over into *naïveté*. But Luciani's praise of conversation was not just a literary device: it became a fundamental attitude and entered into his understanding of the gospels. 'Have you ever thought,' he asked in his letter to Belli, 'why Jesus made his deepest revelations to his disciples while they were sitting at table?'

Venice has always been an international city and the home of many expatriates. Georges Sand was rowed down the Grand Canal in tight trousers, Orson Welles once propped up Harry's Bar, and poor Rolfe alternated between dreams of papal grandeur – he wrote *Hadrian VII* there – and the pursuit of small boys. Nowadays it is a city of tourism and conventions. As Patriarch, Luciani used to attend them whenever he could. After the restoration of the church dei Mendicoli, done at the expense of UNESCO, he shook hands with the builders, workers, architects and scholars who had worked on the project. He even managed to address them in English, a painful, halting, rather punctilious English that he had learned from books rather than travel. They applauded him vigorously. He was always ready to try out his English. In June 1978 a party of English tourists, led by the rural dean of Shrewsbury, Ralph Lumley, attended the feast of St Peter in the church of San Pietro in Castello. Luciani was introduced to them all beforehand, mentioned the 'Anglican Christians' in his sermon, and provided them with a brief summary of his sermon in English before delivering it in Italian. (The three points were: 'My God, I believe in thee; my God, I hope in thee; my God, I love thee.') His palace provided hospitality for two ARCIC meetings, as already mentioned, and for four meetings with the Orthodox. The international contacts Venice makes possible help to dispel the myth that he 'knew nothing about ecumenism' or 'had never met a Protestant'.

But his main work was in Venice and its hinterland. The temptation of hagiography constantly beckons: but it would be quite misleading to suggest that Luciani's time in Venice was all roses and smiles, all sweetness and light. It was not. He had to do battle on two fronts. He did not like the aquatic pomp and circumstance that the people he called 'the ancients' expected of him. The simplicity that enchanted others disappointed them. And, on the other hand, he became increasingly out of sympathy with the growing leftward trend in Italian Catholicism. The left caused him the more dramatic troubles. In 1970 there were violent strikes at Mestre and Marghera, and Luciani's pleas for patience and 'negotiation round a table' were not appreciated by the militant and politically conscious workers. In 1971 he tried to appeal on behalf of the 270 workers of the Sava factory who had been made redundant: the employers were urged 'never to forget the dignity of their workers' and the workers were exhorted to 'seek for a negotiated solution'. Luciani became the man in the middle who was fired on by both sides. He leaned heavily on the student community (FUCI) of San Trovaso when it came out in favour of divorce during the referendum campaign, and did not admit their argument that Italy had become a pluralist society. He committed himself to the hilt in the election of 15 June 1975: those priests who had suggested that it was permissible for Catholics to vote for left-wing candidates, Communists in short, were brusquely told that such a *scelta di classe*, an option for the working class, would place the liberty of Italy in jeopardy. And in addition to all these difficulties during his time in Venice was the distressing knowledge that there were 107 churches in the city proper, half of which were closed, that those that were open were frequented mostly by tourists and estimable old ladies, and the terrible fear that the Patriarch would be reduced to being a keeper in a vast ecclesiastical museum. For the 'glories' of Venice, as he had hinted in his inaugural sermon, were an ambivalent asset: they were so far in the past that they could heighten the sense of frustration in the present.

It was partly to relieve his frustrations that he began to write *Illustrissimi*, a series of letters to authors or characters in history or fiction. Here is his own explanation: 'When I preach in St Mark's, I have a hundred, a hundred and fifty, at most two hundred listeners. Half of them are tourists who don't understand Italian, and the other half are wonderful people but they are . . .well, getting on in age. Then the editor of the *Messagero di San Antonio* said to me: "Write for us, and your audience will increase a thousandfold." He convinced me' (*Il Tempo*, Rome, 27 August 1978).

It would be absurd to maintain that *Illustrissimi* is a great work of literature or that many people would have read it unless its author had become pope; but it would also be unjust to deny that it is a very good book, judged as an essay in popular communication. It reveals an unstuffy, non-pompous Luciani. Others may write theological treatises, but he writes letters to authors who have become his friends through long frequentation. It is not a work of literary criticism. Very frequently he simply used an author as a peg on which to hang a moral or a religious point. He was interested in the English Elizabethan dramatist Christopher ('Kit') Marlowe, whom he first came to know as a boy through the Italian poet Carducci, because *Doctor Faustus* gave him a chance to speak of the devil. Goethe became an instance of *noblesse oblige*. Chesterton in *The Ball and the Cross* pleased him because he made the point that 'people who begin by despising the cross of Christ end by making the world uninhabitable'. In his letter to Mr Pickwick he used Pickwick's archaeological ruminations on what he thinks is an ancient inscription ('Bill Stumps, his mark') to show how people can be wildly wrong and yet still in good faith.

But the real importance of *Illustrissimi* lay elsewhere. It demonstrated, first of all, the cultural breadth of Luciani and his constant attempt to let theology – better, faith – remain in dialogue with writers, whether believers or not, who have diagnosed the human condition. As he made clear in his letter to the Roman poet Trilussa (1871–1950), the study of literature is part of the preparation for faith, and he insisted that faith is not 'a stroll through pleasant gardens' but a journey that is 'sometimes difficult, often dramatic, and always mysterious'. Secondly, *Illustrissimi* revealed a man with an impatient passion to communicate: Luciani was not someone to leave his treasure wrapped up in a napkin or buried in the ground. Thirdly, it shows someone who could relate the Gospel to everyday things with a skill and perceptiveness that are rare. Karl Rahner, who is mentioned in *Illustrissimi* had theorised abundantly about 'everyday things'. But book for book, Luciani was better at showing how grace penetrates, if we are prepared to let it, into the remotest corners of human existence. The comparison with Rahner was not outlandish: for Rahner has claimed to be a dilettante and he prefers the suggestive essay to the – for the time being – impossible treatise. Fourthly, *Illustrissimi* demonstrated that Luciani was a writer fully in command of his art. He wrote directly, spontaneously, with the apparent ease that comes from hard work over a long period of time. What it cost him was not revealed. Yet he appears as he was in these letters, unbuttoned, with no faking and no pretence. His preferred genre was the informal letter, in which he could let the association of ideas direct his pen.

I have chosen to give a brief account of *Illustrissimi* before discussing his other utterances because it seems to be more typical of the man. Only Luciani among the Italian bishops could have written *Illustrissimi*; almost any Italian bishop could – and no doubt did – make similar speeches warning against 'false pluralism', urging support for the anti-divorce referendum, denouncing 'self-appointed theologians', and so on. The more predictable Luciani was, the less he was interesting. One has to understand, however, the special position of Italian bishops in relation to the Vatican: since the pope is the primate of Italy, he takes a particular interest in the activity of the bishops, and they are expected to support papal policies without reservation. When Bishop Betazzi, of Ivrea, exchanged a series of letters with the communist leader, Berlinguer, he was regarded as having stepped out of line. It was not the sort of indulgence a Patriarch of Venice could permit himself, even supposing that he had wanted to. In 1971 Pope Paul had nominated him as one of the non-elected members of the Synod. In 1972 he became vice-president of the Italian Bishops' Conference (CEI) and held this office for three years. In September 1972 Pope Paul stopped in Venice on his way to the Eucharistic Congress at Undine, and before a vast crowd in St Mark's Square took off his stole and placed it on the shoulders of Luciani ('*Mi ha fatto diventare tutto rosso*' – 'He made me blush', said Luciani at his first Angelus as pope). And at the consistory of 5 March 1973 he was made a cardinal. These growing responsibilities and marks of trust bound him by a special tie of loyalty. Not that there was any duplicity or mental restriction involved: it was simply that the pressures to conform, on someone who was ready to conform, were greater. Pope John as Patriarch of Venice had behaved in exactly the same way: though his personality shone through in his pastoral work, he was obedient to Pius XII as a matter of course. Yet on becoming pope he surprised the world, and for him the petrine office was a liberation. It was as though he had been biding his time.

An anthology of statements from these years could easily be compiled to show that Patriarch Luciani, despite his bright start in Venice, was less open to new ideas than he had been in Vittoria Veneto. The note of warning is constantly being sounded. Dangers are emphasized more than possibilities. He began to write in *Osservatore Romano*. On the Synod he wrote: 'Some have gone so far as to suggest that decisions at the Synod should be taken on the basis of a majority vote. But that would be to apply democratic methods to the Church. The Church, however, is different, and the Synod is not a parliament. The fathers are neither legislating nor decision-making – they are the consultative organ of the pope' (*Osservatore Romano*, 7–8 January 1972). At the 1974 Synod on evangelization, he stressed that although it was true to say that the whole community had the task of evangelization, the words of Christ, 'He who hears you hears me', were addressed to the bishops specifically. He went on: 'There is a lot of superficial writing around today from people who act as though they were teachers in the Church, without bothering to receive a mandate from the *magisterium* or even trying to be in harmony with its teachings.' At the Eucharistic Congress at Pescara in September 1977 he returned to the theme of authority: 'In the modern state authority comes from below, from the people. In the Church it is different. Christ alone confers authority on the pope and the bishops, and also makes clear how it should be exercised. Authority exists for the service of the faithful, entirely and solely for their good, so that they are more younger brothers of the pastors than subjects, responsible crewmen aboard the barque of the Church rather than mere passengers.' The heavy emphasis on authority is no doubt intelligible in the Italian context, where there are so many free-wheeling basic groups which are openly defiant of the institutional Church or stand very loosely towards it or believe that a new, transformed Church is gradually emerging from below (cf. Pietro Brugnoli, 'Scelta socialista ed esperanza di fede', IDOC, November 1974). But many of Luciani's statements reveal an authoritarian desire to restore order, as though he had despaired of relating the stirrings of new life to the Church community.

There were, happily, other strands in the thinking of Patriarch Luciani during these Venice years. Genuine concern for the third world never left him. As we have seen, it was one of the factors in his election. At the 1971 Synod he proposed that the rich churches of the West should systematically give one per cent of their income to the poorer churches of the third world. This could be called, he said, 'the brothers' share', and 'it should not be regarded as alms-giving but as something that was owing as part compensation for the injustices that our consumer society is constantly inflicting on the developing world, and to make reparation for the social sins that should not be glossed over.' With this critique of the consumer society went, logically, his old obsession with poverty in the Church. He wrote to the people of Venice in February 1976:

> I have urged and authorized parish priests to get rid of gold plate, pearls and rings offered by the faithful as ex-votos . . . I want to set an example myself by offering the golden chain which used to belong to Pope Pius XII and which was given to me by Pope John XXIII when he ordained me bishop. It is not much in view of the immensity of the needs. But perhaps it will help to make it understood that the real treasures of the Church are the poor, the disinherited, the weak, and that they should be helped, not by occasional alms-giving, but in such a way that they can rise to the standard of life and the level of education to which they have a right.

The proceeds were to be devoted to the Centro Don Orione for mentally handicapped children. The combination of doctrinal rigour and social open-mindedness is not uncommon among Italian churchmen. It can be a way of masking graver problems. But at least it shows that in Luciani's vision of the Church it is a community of caring and concern.

In his last three years in Venice, Cardinal Luciani began to speak out on every conceivable topic. His old shyness had gone. He rarely refused to write a newspaper article or to give an interview. He used his homilies to speak about topical subjects. He took the risk of commitment. The suggestion (made in *Le Monde*, 29 August 1978) that he kept a low profile and followed the eighteenth century maxim on how to get on in the ecclesiastical career ('Do nothing, while profiting from every occasion that presents itself') is a manifest absurdity. Luciani knew the dilemma that faces many a bishop: if he speaks, he is criticized for what he says; if he says nothing, he is criticized for his silence. He came to prefer the risk of speaking out to the risk of silence.

In what proved to be – though he cannot have known it at the time – his last statement as Patriarch of Venice, he addressed himself to the problem of Louise Brown, Oldham's test-tube baby, who had been conceived with the help of doctors in the laboratory and successfully implanted in her mother's womb. Luciani wrote an article on this subject in the review *Prospettive nel Mondo*. It was reported in advance by ANSA, the Italian news agency (3 August 1978). Luciani said that he shared the enthusiasm for technical progress that had made this birth possible. He congratulated the child and her parents. He wondered about the possibility of abuse of this technique, the risks involved, and whether science might become like the sorcerer's apprentice – controlling rather than controlled. Condemnation was withheld: 'As for the parents, I have no right to condemn them, subjectively, if they acted in good faith and with a right intention, and they may have great merit before the Lord.' He then recalled the teaching of Pius XII who distinguished two cases: first where the medical intervention could be said to 'complete' the sexual act by taking it to its natural conclusion – and that was permissible; and secondly where conception results from the medical intervention in such a way that it becomes a substitute for sexual union, which is not permissible since 'God has linked procreation with married sexuality'. It was a restatement of traditional teaching, though sympathetic in tone. And his concluding remarks were equally traditional and may have a bearing on his attitude to *Humanae Vitae*, which he had also defended: 'As for individual conscience, it must always be followed, but the individual is obliged to have a well-formed conscience.' Firmness on principles combined with an understanding of the problems people actually have: that is one definition of the 'pastoral' approach that Luciani took in moral questions.

Patriarch Luciani left Venice at 6 a.m. on Thursday 10 August. During the pre-conclave period he stayed at the Augustinian house of Saint Monica, 25 via del Sant' Uffizio, on the left of Bernini's colonnade. One of his neighbours there was Cardinal James Darcy Freeman, Archbishop of Sydney. The Augustinians found him friendly, and noted the way he would sit in any place available at the table when he came back late from the General Congregations. But he refused to be drawn on the conclave. Two of the nuns, however, asked him what he thought about newspaper stories on likely candidates and where the journalists got their information from. He did not want to comment, but they insisted that he could reply without breaking the secret. Finally he said: 'Journalists should learn to write less and to pray more.' But he was still thinking about Venice. He had a visit from Giuseppe Bosa, his Vicar General, and they talked about future appointments. His secretary, Don Diego Lorenzi, reported that he spent much of his time preparing a retreat he was due to give on 5 September. Cheerful Brother Clemente of St. Monica's carried his bag across St Peter's Square on the opening day of the conclave. He recalls that he said: 'I don't know what to say, Your Eminence. Best wishes and *arrivederci*. If you are elected pope, come and see us some time. We are neighbours after all.' The only answer was a shy smile.

9

The Thirty-three Day Pope

Every one of us should seek to be good, and to infect others with a goodness that is shot through with the gentleness and love taught by Christ.
                    Pope John Paul I, 24 September 1978

On Sunday 27 August Pope John Paul was about to speak to the people for the first time. After four weeks of limpid blue skies, there were clouds overhead and a few spots of rain at five minutes to noon. But this did nothing to dampen the spirits of the crowd, estimated at 200,000. The mood was festive. A band of the Italian army provided music that was cheerful, if harmonically thin. Then the Pope appeared and the crowd waved hats, handkerchiefs, cameras, copies of the special edition of *Osservatore Romano* with the gold edging designed by Manzu. Children were hoisted onto shoulders so they could get a better view. Nuns looked rapt. John Paul waved cheerfully back at the crowd. His white skullcap was perched uncertainly on the back of his head, and his unruly quiff emerged. As Cardinal Basil Hume later remarked: 'It is always a bit of a winner if you can have your skullcap slightly asquiff – it suggests a degree of incompetence that is not threatening.' His first word – 'Yesterday' – got a laugh, and he paused to relish the moment. He picked up again: 'Yesterday morning I went to the Sistine Chapel to vote peacefully. I never would have imagined what was to take place.' He had not started with any conventional form of address to 'My dear children', and he used the first person singular. The two cardinals who had encouraged him when 'danger' threatened were referred to as 'colleagues', not as 'most eminent cardinals'. There were none of the pompous rolling adjectives so frequent on such occasions. He explained his choice of name, the first double-barrelled name in the history of the papacy:

> As for the choice of name, when they asked me, I had to stop and think a while. My thoughts went like this: Pope John had wanted to consecrate me with his own hands here in the basilica of St Peter's. Then, though unworthy, I succeeded him in the cathedral of St Mark – in that Venice that is still filled with the spirit of Pope John. The gondoliers remember him, the sisters, everyone. On the other hand, Pope Paul not only made me a cardinal, but some months before that, in St Mark's Square, he made me blush in front of 20,000 people, because he took off his stole and placed it on my shoulders. I was never so red-faced. Furthermore, in the fifteen years of his pontificate, this pope showed not only me but the whole world how he loved the Church, how he served it, worked for it, and suffered for this Church of Christ. And so I took the name 'John Paul'.
>
> Be sure of this. I do not have the wisdom of heart of Pope John. I do not have the preparation and culture of Pope Paul. However, I now stand in their place. I will seek to serve the Church and hope you will help me with your prayers.

This direct homely style worked. The crowd slowly dispersed, moved, and in good humour. Pope John Paul had had about fifteen minutes in which to choose a name. The first pope to change his name was Sergius IV (1009–1012) who needed to get away from his unfortunate nickname, *Os Porci* ('Old Pigface'). In modern times the choice of a name had been a declaration of policy. Roncalli broke with the long line of Piuses by taking the slightly shady name – in papal history – of John. And Montini said something about his missionary hopes by taking the name Paul.

By choosing the name John Paul, Luciani was saying that he would pursue a policy of continuity; but as John Paul I (a convention that is not normally used until there is a second of the same name), he was hinting that it would be continuity with a difference. But Giovanni Paolo was rather cumbersome in Italian, and Romans soon abbreviated it to the more familiar and friendly Gianpaolo.

But already that same morning John Paul had given a more substantial account of his intentions in a speech to the cardinals during the Mass at 9.30 a.m. This was another departure from precedent. The Pope had been up most of the night, still in cell No. 60, in order to write his speech. This speed off the mark indicated that John Paul wanted to share with the cardinals who had elected him an outline of his thoughts on the way the Church should go. He was a pope in a hurry. His speech fell naturally into four parts: the awesome burden of the office, the nature of the Church, the six-point programme, and greetings to various categories. I will concentrate on the two middle sections.

Pope John Paul saw the Church not as existing for its own sake but rather 'at the service of the world'. He stressed this point twice. He pledged to put all his strength 'at the service of the universal mission of the Church, that is to say, at the service of the world'. And he invited all Christians to pledge themselves in the same way: 'The Gospel calls all of us its children to place their full strength, indeed their life, at the service of mankind in the name of the charity of Christ.' At the same time, the service of the world does not mean conformity to it: there is the task of prophetic protest. The Church is in the world and for the world but not of the world. This passage was clinched by a quotation from the constitution *On the Church* which speaks of the Church as 'entering human history' and acting as the 'visible sacrament of saving unity' (9).

He then stressed the uniqueness and irreplaceable nature of the Church (and by Church he clearly meant the Catholic Church). Some ecumenists were distressed by the quotation from St Augustine: 'Only in the Church is salvation: without it one perishes.' But the distress was premature. Later on he spoke of the progress made 'in the relationship between the churches of various denominations'. Their ecclesial reality was recognized. But he had in view the 'uniqueness of the Catholic Church' with its 'tremendous spiritual power'. This spiritual power was needed in the arid wasteland of contemporary culture. Here Pope John Paul briefly developed a theme that had been a constant of his preaching in Venice:

> The world knows well . . . that the sublime perfection which it has attained by scientific research and technology has already reached a peak, beyond which yawns the abyss, blinding the eyes with darkness . . . The danger facing modern man is that he would reduce the earth to a desert, the person to an automaton, brotherly love to planned collectivization, often introducing death where God wishes life.

He left his hearers to spell out the precise nature of these perils, but it is not unreasonable to suppose that he was thinking about ecology, nuclear weapons, the all-powerful state, and abortion.

He promised a pontificate in continuity with his predecessors – reaching back as far as Pius XI. But, he went on, 'the pastoral plan of Pope Paul VI, our immediate predecessor, has most of all left a strong impression on our heart and in our memory.'

So he reached his programme. In view of his emphasis on continuity, it could hardly be startlingly original. But the order of priorities was not without interest. First came the continuing implementation of Vatican II, which should proceed without 'hesitation or timidity'. Second was the revision of the code of canon law for the Oriental and the Western Churches. He said: 'We wish to preserve the integrity of the great discipline of the Church in the life of priests and faithful'. If that sounded rather ominous, one should remember that the framework of law in the Church can be releasing as much as constricting, and Pope John Paul suggested this by speaking in the same paragraph of 'the blessed liberty of the children of God'. The third plank of the programme was evangelization understood as a task for 'all the sons and daughters of the Church'. The fourth was ecumenism, which would be pursued in the spirit of Christ's priestly prayer, 'That all may be one' (John 17: 21). Despite the progress made,

> Division remains a cause for concern, and indeed a contradiction and a scandal in the eyes of non-Christians and non-believers. We intend to dedicate our prayerful attention to everything that would favour union. We will do so without diluting doctrine but, at the same time, without hesitation.

The fifth point was about dialogue with all men. He would follow the principle stated in *Ecclesiam Suam*, 'namely, that men, as men, should know one another, even those who do not share our faith'. Finally he stressed that work for peace would continue, in collaboration with anyone who cared to join in:

> We call upon all good men, all who are just, honest and true. We ask them to build up a dam within their nations against blind violence which can only destroy and sow seeds of ruin and sorrow.

The structure of the programme was clear and logical: he moved from considering the Church 'in itself' towards looking at it in its relationships.

The greetings filled out what was lacking in the programme. The greeting to bishops gave him a chance to say that he had a high regard for collegiality: 'We value their efforts in the guidance of the universal Church and the curial structure in which they share by right according to the norms established.' Young people were hailed as 'the hope of tomorrow', and families as 'the domestic church'.

Finally he greeted 'the suffering, the sick, prisoners, exiles, the unemployed, those who are down on their luck'. The Lebanon, the Holy Land, and 'the troubled land of India', recently devastated by floods, were mentioned by name.

This speech – delivered within sixteen hours of his election was to prove the most important act of the pontificate. He had not burned the midnight oil in vain. In retrospect it could be taken as his last will and testament to the Church. But in the immediate it was regarded as Pope John Paul's way of thanking the cardinals who had elected him; and since in the end he had had virtually unanimous support, the bouquets were scattered around liberally in every direction. Cardinal Felici was pleased with the high priority given to the revision of the code of canon law. Conservatives would be happy with the warning about too much latitude in the interpretation of conciliar texts and the promise of doctrinal firmness in ecumenism. European progressives, on the other hand, could counter that he saw the Council as energizing the Church, committed himself strongly on ecumenism, and made friendly noises about collegiality and the Synod. Third world cardinals noted the emphasis on human rights and international justice. But the difficulty of facing all ways at once and being all things to all men was immediately apparent. One waited apprehensively for the first crisis, little imagining that it would be his death.

But this was the honeymoon period, and Pope John Paul had a good press. Only Andrew Young, U.S. Ambassador to UNO, said that he thought the appointment was a mistake and that he would have preferred someone from the third world. And the Soviet news agency, Tass, reported the election in three miserly lines. Even the Chinese did better than that, though the millions of China learned about the death of Pope Paul only when the news of his successor was announced. The Polish news agency, PAP, supplied a full biography and stressed that he was 'the first working-class pope'. The rest of the world tried to cope with its surprise, and was prepared to give the unknown Luciani the benefit of the doubt. Something of the euphoria of the cardinals was communicated to the media. But in the general atmosphere of optimism, a few dissenting voices could be heard. Richard P. McBrien, professor of theology at Boston College, was less than enthusiastic (he was probably writing before the conclave, but that does not affect the principle). His view was that a smiling, reconciling pope who stressed continuity – as the conventional wisdom demanded – would 'only intensify the frustrations of both left and right alike'. He went on:

> What the Catholic Church needs now is a shaking down and a sorting out. If Providence has her on a conservative course, then let that become unmistakably clear under the new pope so that those who cannot abide such a course will be able to pursue other options for the sake of God's Kingdom without further delay. And if Providence has a more progressive course for the Church, then let *that* be unmistakably clear so that those who could not really accept Vatican II and have been waiting for the day of its effective repeal will be free to pursue the holy grail of orthodoxy in some other Christian household ('Agenda for the Papacy' in *Commonweal*, 1 September 1978).

McBrien's remedy for the situation was threefold: revoke the anti-contraception teaching of *Humanae Vitae*, abolish obligatory celibacy for priests, and set in motion 'forces that will lead eventually to the full incorporation of qualified women to priestly and episcopal ministry'. Charles Davis' contribution to the same number of *Commonweal* was to call for the dismantling of something called 'the Vatican power structure', and Leonard Swidler hoped that the scandal of a super-secret conclave would never happen again, and that the college of cardinals would be – a sinister term from Orwell's *1984* – 'eliminated'.

Response to the election obviously depended upon previous expectations, and it was difficult to think of a candidate who would have fulfilled the hopes of the *Commonweal* writers, still less how he could have gained the votes needed to win the contest. But what was more evident in the via della Conciliazione than in Madison Avenue, was that Pope John Paul, if not actually about to inaugurate instant *parousia*, would spring a modest surprise or two. In his first week he gave audiences on successive days to the cardinals, the diplomats accredited to the Holy See and to journalists.

There werè 88 cardinals still left in Rome on Wednesday 23 August. At 11 a.m. they assembled in the Hall of the Consistory. Cardinal Confalonieri presented their greetings in the ornate manner that is his wont: all his adjectives were superlatives, and he twice referred to 'the august pontiff'. But 'the august pontiff' was beginning to find all this ceremony a little tiresome, and abandoned his set speech on the grounds that it was 'too curial in style'. He preferred to speak from the heart. His prepared text – certainly not written by him – solemnly referred to the indebtedness of the entire Church to the Roman Curia whose role was 'to assure the organic articulation of legitimate autonomies, while respecting the need for essential unity and discipline'. What he actually said was: 'As soon as I had a little time, the first thing I did on becoming pope was to get hold of the *Annuario Pontificio* and study the organization of the Holy See.' Though that did not suggest that he was on the verge of dismantling the Curia, it was at least put in its place. He also essayed one of his baroque comparisons. The Church was like a clock. Its hands give guidance to the world; but it has to be wound up, and that is the task of the Curia. The official texts put out by the Vatican press office and *Osservatore Romano* ignored all these off-the-cuff remarks and restored the pontifical 'we'. Already Romans began to talk about 'the censored pope'.

The address to diplomats on 31 August was naturally a more formal affair. The cardinals had deliberately chosen a 'pastoral' rather than a 'diplomatic' pope, and yet the international role of the Vatican still remained. John Paul confessed his ignorance of international politics and his inexperience, but he saw two levels on which the Church could work with the nations. First, through participation in international organizations 'in the search for better solutions to great problems such as *détente*, disarmament, peace, justice, humanitarian measures and aid, development and so on.' The second level of activity was more directly pastoral. Through its teaching the Church can help to form consciences, 'chiefly the consciences of Christians but also of those men and women of good will, and through them forming a wider public opinion on the fundamental principles that guarantee authentic civilization and real brotherhood between peoples.'

Pope Paul had always been at home with diplomats: he was one of them. Pope John Paul seemed much more relaxed with the 800 journalists whom he entertained the following day (1 September). With his skullcap still slightly askew and the quiff of hair obstinately emerging, he padded energetically into the Hall of Benedictions to thank the press for the 'sacrifices and labours of August' and to promise them in the future 'a special, frank, honest and effective collaboration'. Cynical journalists – there are a few – had heard that before. But he soon had them eating out of his hand. He reported the remark of Cardinal Mercier to the editor of *La Croix*: 'Today, St Paul would be a journalist'. 'No,' said the editor, 'he would be the director of Reuter's' (scowls from UPI, AP and Agence France Presse). Pope John Paul added: 'I think St Paul would not only be head of Reuter's but would also ask for a little time on television.' The notion that Cardinal Mercier or a long-lost editor of *La Croix* could be a guide to the theology of the media in the age of Marshall McLuhan may have seemed rather quaint, but that could be an instance of cultural chauvinism. His frame of reference was Italian. He quoted, for instance, the remark of an Italian editor who told his reporters that the public was not interested in what Napoleon III said to William of Prussia, but rather whether their socks were beige or red and whether they smoked cigarettes or not. Everybody laughed, but they may at the same time have had a lingering feeling that sometimes 'colour' or 'human interest' may be more revealing than the self-important exchanges of those who presume to carve up the world and to determine its future. Tucked in between the anecdotes and familiar reminiscences was a more solemn exhortation: 'I ask you to maintain a profound consideration for the things of God and the mysterious relationship between God and each one of us.' In other words, there are more things in heaven and earth than are dreamt of, even by the head of Reuter's.

But Pope John Paul did not devote the entire week to talk. He also acted and confirmed the heads of Roman dicasteries or departments in their offices. Or more precisely he 'nominated' Cardinal Jean Villot as Secretary of State, and 'reconfirmed' the others. The confidence shown in Villot was important: it meant that Pope John Paul was prepared to trust a man who had his critics in the Curia. It was also an acknowledgement of the way Villot had fulfilled his task as camerlengo in the preparation of the conclave. The 'reconfirmation' of the remaining 17 heads of curial departments was a gesture towards continuity: Pope John Paul's study of the *Annuario Pontificio*, combined with what was common knowledge in Rome, must have shown him that three cardinals (Seper, Wright and Garrone) had already expressed a desire to resign on grounds of ill-health, and that five more had already exceeded the official five-year stint (Baggio, Philippe, Pignedoli, Willebrands and Paupini). The remaining nine would have to offer their resignations within two to four years. But they were all 'reconfirmed'.

One other decision was less popular with the Curia. There is traditionally a new pope's bounty received by all its members. The first instalment comes automatically on the death of a pope, and the second on the election of a new pope. The first bonus was paid as usual, but Pope John Paul cut the second instalment by half: instead of the customary one month's salary (about £250 or $500) they received only £125 or $250. The exact financial situation of the Vatican remains a closely guarded secret, despite talk of openness in the past decade, and it seems that inflation has hit the Holy See as much as the members of the E.E.C. That there was a genuine concern about the financial losses of the Vatican was hinted at by Cardinal Cordeiro of Karachi in a pre-conclave interview when he said that 'there were certain matters that cardinals could not even talk to bishops about' (Interview with Kevin O'Kelly, RTE, Dublin).

But such recondite affairs did not bother the Roman crowd. At his second Angelus appearance on 3 September, Pope John Paul confirmed the good impression made the previous Sunday. He began by quoting a Venetian saying that 'Every good thief has his particular devotion'. His own, he explained, was for St Gregory the Great, whose feast it happened to be. The seminary in Belluno, with which he had been associated for 27 years, first as student and then as professor, was dedicated to St Gregory. He recalled Gregory's love of the poor, his reluctance to become pope, and his memorable remark that 'the emperor wants a monkey to become a lion'.

Lions had been worrying him in another way. He wanted to include in his coat of arms a reminiscence of both Pope John and Pope Paul. Pope Paul was recalled in the symbolic mountains he had already used in Venice (but they became *montini*, the hills of Rome), and Pope John was commemorated in the lion of St Mark. There remained the three five-pointed stars, representing faith, hope and charity, on an azure background, as his own contribution. Archbishop Bruno Heim, Apostolic Delegate in London and an authority on heraldry, was responsible for the design and earnestly conferred by telephone with the *sostituto*, Mgr Caprio. The coat of arms was surmounted by the crossed keys and tiara. ('Even if he was not crowned,' observed Archbishop Heim, 'the tiara remains on his coat of arms. And I noticed during the television that he had it on his mitre during the ceremony.') There ensued a brisk exchange of letters in *The Times* of London about why the crossed keys were identical:

surely the keys of heaven and of hell could not be the same, correspondents wrote. Milton was evoked. Various fantastic explanations were suggested: they were both keys of heaven, suggested someone, because the gates of hell cannot be unlocked from the outside.

But the abandonment of the tiara was perhaps a more serious matter than Archbishop Heim, a disappointed herald, was prepared to allow. It signified in as clear a way as possible the final relinquishing of the temporal claims of the papacy. Like the 'keys of St Peter', the tiara had been mythologized to a remarkable degree. Of Asiatic origin, it symbolized regal power, and was wholly unsuited to 'the servant of the servants of God'. Bismarck, on hearing that it represented authority over heaven, hell and earth, is reported to have said that he was prepared to leave the first two realms to the pope, but not the third. Throughout John Paul's first week there had been intense discussion about what to call the ceremony by which he officially became pope. Since he refused to be 'crowned', there could be no question of 'coronation' (though the term was used in *Romano Pontifici Eligendo*, No. 92). 'Enthronement' was briefly toyed with, but he did not want that either. The tiara, the waving ostrich plumes, even the *sedia gestatoria* – all were to be relegated to the Vatican lumber room. But in all this Pope John Paul was not simply giving another demonstration of his 'humility'. He was rather making a point about the Petrine office itself. All the titles that theologians had criticized as unscriptural or even pagan – Vicar of Christ, Supreme Pontiff, Head of the Church – were abandoned in favour of pope, bishop of Rome, supreme pastor. What happened, therefore, at 6 p.m. on the evening of 3 September, anniversary of the outbreak of the Second World War, was simply 'the inauguration of his ministry as supreme pastor'.

Pope John Paul received the pallium from Cardinal Felici. The trappings of temporal power had been replaced by this eminently Christian symbol. The pallium has been presented to metropolitan archbishops, of both East and

West, from the fourth century. It is made of lamb's wool presented to the pope on the feast of St Agnes: it is therefore linked with pastoral care. It is placed over the shoulders and resembles a yoke: it is a reminder that the service of unity will not be easy, but that the burden borne by the Christian is, with the help of the Lord, light. Finally, it is presented to the metropolitan and to the pope as coming 'from the tomb of St Peter': thus all stewardship in the Church is connected with the founding apostle. To the millions watching on television, the splendid setting of St Peter's Square, theatrical and intended to be so, was becoming familiar. They had seen Pope Paul's funeral. But now instead of a plain coffin there was a smiling pope who embraced the cardinals on both cheeks and chatted away with each of them in turn. Some of his words were recorded. 'Don't forget', he told Cardinal Hume, 'that I'm relying on the prayers of British Catholics.' Cardinal Bernard Alfrink of Holland had trouble with his knees and could not kneel, but that made no difference. Last of all came one of the over-eighties, Cardinal Slipyi, the would-be patriarch of the Ukrainian Catholic Church, in his stove-pipe hat. The Sistine Chapel choir insisted on singing, endlessly, the verse 'Thou art Peter and upon this rock I will build my Church'. This triumphalism seemed out of harmony with the rest of the ceremony, and with Pope John Paul's homily, started in Latin, continued in French and concluded in his lilting Veneto Italian. He presented himself as 'presiding over the community of charity' and spoke warmly of 'the Christian brothers not yet in full communion with us'. Darkness fell before the end of the ceremony. The television lights became useful. The nights were getting longer.

After his inauguration Pope John Paul tore into 'the presidency of charity' with a zest that was positively alarming in a man who, as he told one of his Wednesday audiences, had been in hospital eight times and had had four operations. There was a sad and dramatic moment on Tuesday 5 September when Metropolitan Nikodim of Leningrad, the man who had done more than anyone else on the Russian side to foster good relations with the Catholic Church, died suddenly in the Pope's study. There were speeches, speeches, all personally written. He talked to a group of American bishops on 21 September on one of his favourite topics: the family as 'the domestic church', a church in miniature, and the parents as 'the first and best catechists'. On 23 September he emerged from the Vatican – for the first and last time – to take possession of his cathedral of St John Lateran. Again the style was different. Instead of being carried across the city on the *sedia gestatoria* he was driven over in an open car with as few outriders as possible. But he made a concession to tradition and popular demand by mounting the *sedia* when he reached the basilica: people said they wanted to see him. In his homily he somewhat surprisingly denounced false notions of liturgical 'creativity' which had led to excesses. One was not aware that this was the most urgent problem of the diocese of Rome. But next morning, speaking from his window, he was positive again and talked about 'the contagious power of goodness'. The pontificate was galloping along. But he admitted to Cardinal Villot that he was finding it a heavy burden (*'une charge très lourde'*). The words he had spoken in his programmatic speech to the cardinals had not been mere conventional rhetoric: 'If our unaided human strength cannot be equal to this heavy responsibility, the omnipotent help of God who guides his Church through the centuries, through so many conflicts and troubles, will certainly not abandon us, the humble and most recent "servant of the servants of God"'.

God responded to this trust in his own disconcerting way. On Friday 29 September came the stunning announcement that Pope John Paul had been found dead at 5.30 a.m. Fr John Magee, who had been kept on as English-language secretary, became worried when the Pope did not appear for Mass as usual. He went to his room, found him dead in bed, with the lights still on and à Kempis' *Imitation of Christ* by the bedside. His doctor was called and concluded that death of a massive heart attack must have occurred at about

11 p.m. the previous night. The shock was all the greater because he had appeared so fit and ebullient at his public audience that very day. He had also spoken to a group of bishops from the Philippines, and warned them that they must preach the spiritual ideals of Christianity as well as trying to alleviate poverty and misery. At 10 p.m., as he prepared to go to bed, he was given the news of the murder of a left-wing youth in Rome, and said, softly, 'Even young people are killing each other now . . . .' Those were his last recorded words. The man who had loved people and conversation died alone, without the sacraments of the Church, unable to communicate with anyone except God. As the news of his death spread, there was a feeling of numbed and uncomprehending shock. The most garrulous had nothing to say. The analysis of his brief and hectic pontificate now seemed trivial compared with the silencing of his voice and the extinction of his smile. There were memories, but they were a poor substitute for the vivid presence of the man. Rejoicing had so quickly and un-expectedly turned to mourning.

It is not unfair to the memory of **Pope Paul** to say that his successor's death was felt as a more grievous blow. After all, Pope Paul had had fifteen years to leave his mark on the papacy, and his death, though unexpected in its timing, was not a surprise. Pope John Paul's death, on the other hand, was harder to bear, and the grief was more profound. It was as though a vision of hope and reconciliation had been tantalizingly glimpsed and then suddenly dashed to the ground. As his body lay in state in the Sala Clementina and, from Saturday 30 September, in St Peter's, an endless crowd of mourners passed by, and this time many of them wept openly. Romans outnumbered tourists. The body already seemed smaller than one remembered him, and the face had a greyish pallor. His red shoes showed scarcely any signs of wear. At his inauguration he had abolished the ceremony in which two Franciscans used to tend smoking flax and utter the dire warning: *'Sic transit gloria mundi'* ('Thus does the world's glory pass'). His funeral was fixed for Wednesday 4 October, feast of St Francis the patron of Italy.

Don Diego Lorenzi, Pope John Paul's other private secretary, had thoughtfully telephoned the family in Canale d'Agordo before the news was officially released. At 6.20 in the morning of 29 September he spoke to the Pope's niece, Pia, daughter of Edoardo and wife of a meat salesman. He came straight to the point: '*Zio Albino è morto*' ('Uncle Albino is dead'). Pia dressed and drove down with her husband and two children to the baroque chuch in Canale d'Agordo. The parish priest, Don Rinaldo Andrich, had just finished Mass and the congregation of thirty was still in the church. Pia whispered to him the same message: 'Uncle Albino is dead.' He turned to the congregation and said: 'They tell me the Pope is dead.' He couldn't think of anything else to say. Edoardo, meanwhile, was in Australia, engaged upon an export drive. He had been 'the Pope's brother' for thirty-three days.

10

Once more unto the Breach

We shall not cease from exploration
And the end of all our exploring
Will be to arrive where we started
And know the place for the first time.
T. S. Eliot, 'The Four Quartets', in *Collected Poems 1909–1962* (Faber and Faber, London, 1963, p. 222)

The funeral of Pope John Paul I was a damp affair. Bishops and diplomats emptied the pools of water off their green plastic chairs before gingerly sitting down shortly before 4 p.m. The diplomatic representation was less exalted than at the funeral of Pope Paul VI. The Secretariat of State had let it be known that statesmen would not be expected to disrupt their plans for the third time within a few weeks. It was hoped that they would come to the inauguration of the new pope, whenever he was elected. From the top of Bernini's colonnade one saw a mass of black umbrellas. The cardinals, meanwhile, got stoically soaked. Cardinal Confalonieri, who presided at the Mass, was protected by a canopy held over the altar. It would no doubt have made more sense to have held the Requiem Mass inside St Peter's: but the desire to allow as many people as possible to take part justified the risk with the weather. More than one journalist permitted himself to say that 'even the heavens wept'. And the rain stopped just in time for communion.

There were ninety-five cardinals present. The other sixteen would soon arrive. This time they were in a hurry. At the second General Congregation, entry into the conclave was fixed for 14 October, the earliest possible date. The reason was obvious. Too many previous appointments had been broken, too many arrangements had been wrecked, for any cardinal to want to linger in Rome longer than was strictly necessary. Puebla, the CELAM meeting which had been so carefully prepared and so intensely criticized, was postponed *sine die*. Secondly, there was a feeling that this time they were no longer novices who did not know each other very well. They were now old hands who had gone over this course successfully already. Cardinal John J. Carberry of St Louis expressed this optimistic mood when he said that in August, 'We felt as though we were going into a dark tunnel; now it is as though we are entering a bright room.' There was some literal truth in this: the conclave area was somewhat extended and now at least some windows could be opened. And it was less hot. But on the other hand, there was also a burden of sadness at the loss of Pope John Paul I and the summary ending of a pontificate that had seemed so full of promise and hope. This was expressed by Cardinal Basil Hume in his sermon in the church of San Silvestro on Wednesday 11 October, just three days before the conclave: 'We may have been tempted to think that with him we were burying, too, many of our hopes and expectations.' That temptation, certainly, weighed heavily on the pre-conclave period, and contributed to a mood of caution and tentativeness.

For although the same cast of cardinals had assembled on the same baroque stage – they numbered 111 once more since Cardinal John J. Wright, in his wheel-chair, replaced the missing Luciani – and the same chorus of commentators and pressure groups had gathered in Rome, it was obvious that the scenario could not be the same. There were a number of reasons for this. The first was that the whirlwind pontificate of Pope John Paul I had made such a striking impact on the world, that any reversion to the old list of candidates – the unsuccessful names of August – would have produced a feeling of let-down and disappointment. They were already yesterday's men or, in the cruel Italian word, *brucciati*, spent forces. Furthermore, Pope John Paul I had been elected – or so it seemed – for his pastoral qualities and his ability to get on with people and talk to them, and the wisdom of this choice had been powerfully vindicated. His election had been a surprise: but the October conclave could not simply go for the candidate who most resembled Luciani. In any case the supply of Italian 'pastoral' cardinals was not unlimited. If there were to be another surprise, it would have to be a *different kind of surprise.* Fr Andrew Greeley neglected this principle when he fed into his computer in Chicago the requirements that had dominated the August conclave. The computer offered the following list, in order: Ursi of Naples closely followed by Pappalardo of Palermo, Willebrands of Utrecht, Baggio of the Congregation of Bishops and Hume of Westminster. The name of Wojtyla was not fed into the computer, as Greeley later admitted. The political repercussions of an East European pope seemed to exclude him.

But a non-Italian pope was by no means excluded. Pope John Paul I himself, it will be recalled, had said that the time was ripe for a third world pope, and had consistently voted for Cardinal Aloisio Lorscheider in the August conclave. Was it sentimental to think that the cardinals would heed this message from the tomb of the man who now lay buried in the crypt of St Peter's? But his early death was also a warning against choosing someone whose health was fragile, and Lorscheider, though only 53, was known to have had open-heart surgery and to be equipped with a pacemaker. This, in itself, did not rule him out – those who have had open-heart surgery can emerge fitter than before – but it made for caution. Another message from the recent past was now recalled. Cardinal Bernadin Gantin, from the People's Republic of Benin, had been greeted by Pope John Paul I along with the other cardinals during the inauguration Mass. His name means 'Tree of Iron', and Pope John Paul alluded to this as he embraced him and said: 'You are young, you are strong, you will be able to help us.'

There was another voice from the tomb. In *Illustrissimi* Cardinal Luciani had discussed, in his letter to St Bernard of Clairvaux, a deadlocked conclave of the twelfth century to which St Bernard had written a decisive letter (number 24 in his *Opera Omnia*). There were three candidates, a holy man, a learned man and a prudent man. St Bernard had written: 'Let the holy man pray for us sinners; let the learned man write a book that will enlighten our minds; and let the prudent man rule over us – *iste nos regat*.' Luciani then presented a mini-treatise on the virtue of prudence, the only virtue that can be developed by experience. Oddly enough, Cardinal Basil Hume recounted this same story on the day after the election of Pope John Paul II, but he attributed it to an eighteenth century General Congregation of the Jesuits. Mildly challenged on this point, he replied that I should write a learned footnote. That duty is now done.

However, the college of cardinals is a hard-headed body which is not prone to a superstitious reverence for the *obiter dicta* or random sayings of a deceased pope. But the experience of August would most certainly have made them aware that many of the most talented among their number were men in their fifties; and this fact, allied to the evident truth that the papal office has now become a crushing burden, inclined them to look again at the group that included Lorscheider, Gantin, Hume, Benelli, Pappalardo and Wojtyla. They were looking for someone who would not drop down dead. True, the old objections against a long pontificate remained; and the memory of Pio Nono, elected in 1846 at the age of 54, remained as a solemn warning – his thirty-two year pontificate, which began so brightly, had endured to become an embarrassment to the Church. That was why there was renewed interest in the idea of the pope being elected for a limited term or – if that idea seemed too radical a departure from precedent – in a pope who would be prepared to resign.

From this point of view, and despite his reluctance to learn Italian, the name of Cardinal Hume re-appeared on the lists. For when he became Archbishop of Westminster in 1976 – another surprise – he had intimated his intention of resigning after ten years, on the sensible grounds that by then he would have exhausted his stock of imagination and done most of the good of which he was capable. There was every reason to suppose that he would adopt the same approach if called   a prospect which he dreaded   to the papal office. Moreover there would not be the same re-entry problems for a Benedictine ex-pope, who could return with relief to some congenial abbey where he could live out his days in prayer, perhaps writing his memoirs and doing a little quiet fishing. *The Times* of London strongly supported his candidature in a leading article, and used an intriguing anti-Benelli argument: if Pope Paul VI and Benelli had been unable to maintain control of the runaway Church of the 1970s, then Benelli alone could not be expected to pull off this feat. The time had come for a move towards a more collegial style of government in the Church. Cardinal Hume said that he agreed with this editorial, except for the final paragraph in which his own name was put forward. *The Guardian* went even further and on the eve of the conclave predicted that Cardinal Hume would be elected. 'One name was on everyone's lips,' said the page one lead story on 14 October.

But even these splendid newspapers   the thunderer and the gadfly   did not have a vote in the conclave, and more careful attention to what the cardinals were actually saying would have suggested that their minds were working along quite different lines. There was a remarkable unanimity   the effect more of spontaneously working together than of any conspiracy   which led them to re-define the concept of 'pastoral'. True, in August they had sought for and found a 'pastoral' man, and in their August scheme of things 'pastoral' clearly meant 'coming from a diocese'. But then, in October, they tumbled over each other in their anxiety to explain that this was too narrow a definition. Cardinal John J. Krol of Philadelphia insisted that those who worked in diocesan marriage tribunals or the Roman Rota should not be thought of as bureaucrats simply because they dealt with canon law; no, they were profoundly pastoral men since they had to handle intractable human situations in their day-to-day work. Cardinal John Dearden of Detroit made the

same point in the same words, and expressed his compassion
for those who had to work in the Roman Curia. It was left
to Cardinal Gantin to broaden the scope of the term still
more widely. 'All the cardinals,' he chivalrously explained
in the week before the conclave, 'are in some sense pastoral
men, and many of them have administered a diocese – including myself.' And even those whose experience had been
entirely confined to diplomacy or administration had carried
out their work 'in a pastoral way'. Pope Pius XII, it was
recalled, had never been the bishop of a diocese, but that
had not prevented him from being a 'pastoral' pope.

Thus 'pastoral' became a broken-backed word. If it
applied to all 111 cardinals indiscriminately, then it was
useless as a criterion for determining what they might do this
time. One was back once more with uncertainty and darkness, as *Sotto Voce*, an honest man, confessed.

Nevertheless there was one important clue, and it was
provided by the *Novemdiales* sermons which again formed
part of the curial campaign to shape the thinking of the
cardinal electors. We have already seen the important role
played by Cardinal Confalonieri in the August conclave. His
sermon at Pope John Paul I's funeral, though it dwelt
lovingly on the smile which hung about his lips even in death,
endeavoured to interpret the deep inner meaning for the
Church of this all too brief pontificate which he compared
to 'a meteor which unexpectedly lights up the heavens, and
then disappears'. Pope John Paul I, he said, had stressed
'the integrity of faith, the perfection of Christian life, and
the great discipline of the Church'. It sounded vague enough,
but Confalonieri explained it by saying that Pope John
Paul I had already begun to apply these principles to the
government of the diocese of Rome. When he took possession
of his cathedral church of St John Lateran on 23 September,
he showed clearly that he meant to put a stop to liturgical
abuses and would maintain sound doctrine. It was this
insistence on doctrinal rigour which, according to Confalonieri, explained his success with the crowds. It was not
so much the famous smile that drew them as a deep hunger

for the nourishment of solid spirituality: 'Was it the need for spirituality, now more deeply felt because of the neglect of spiritual values, that drew the multitudes towards the pope? How else can one explain the very crowded audiences of Wednesday?' How else, indeed?

At the same time, some observers thought that Pope John Paul I had bungled the visit to St John Lateran. Many people had come in from the shanty towns to see the pope who was said to be the friend of the poor and of whom they had heard so much good. They were disappointed that the Mass was said in Latin, a language that they do not understand, and disconcerted by the denunciation of the sort of liturgy they had in their improvised churches. To hand over £70,000 for the building of a new church in the suburb of Castel Giubileo was all very well, but they were not all that sure that they needed a church. It is only when you have a house that you can start thinking about a church. The Church is first of all the gathered community. It is people.

Such radical and subversive thoughts were far from the mind of Cardinal Giuseppe Siri, Archbishop of Genoa. His packet of votes gained in the August conclave now made him a figure to be reckoned with; and he had also gained a reputation for sagacity because of his warning about not leaving everything to the Holy Spirit. In his sermon on 5 October he paid respect to the inscrutable mysteries of divine providence, but immediately added: 'However it [this death] is not a complete mystery, nor is the event totally opaque. In thirty-four days this pontiff completed his mission.' This was one way of justifying the ways of God to man, and it became the standard form in and around the conclave. Cardinal Carberry said: 'His work was finished, and the Lord took him away.' And Cardinal Timothy Manning of Los Angeles said: 'He made his statement – and then dropped off the stage.' All these remarks, however, seemed to carry the implication that Pope John Paul I might not have turned out to be such a good pope after all, and that by gathering him to himself, the Lord in his wisdom had spared the Church unmentionable disasters. At any rate, the disproportion between the duration of the pontificate and its influence became a favourite theme. *The Tablet* quoted the dictum of St John of the Cross: 'One instant of pure love is worth all the works of the Church put together' (7 October 1978).

The pontificate of Pope John Paul I, then, though brief, was not unfulfilled. Never had so much been accomplished in so short a time. We can now return to Cardinal Siri's sermon:

> With his style so close to the Gospel, it can be said that Pope John Paul I opened an era. He opened it and then quietly went away. In all simplicity he spoke on the firmness of Catholic doctrine, on ecclesiastical discipline, on spirituality which is the basis of the value of human existence. He affirmed that there is a hierarchy in these things – first the grace which comes from God and then the logic that we must never abandon – and then he was silent. The people understood and loved him.

Cardinal Siri's logic was not easy to follow. One expected rather more on the new era of evangelical simplicity inaugurated by Pope John Paul I: that was, after all, his most lasting achievement. But ignoring this, Cardinal Siri swept swiftly on to the familiar themes of sound doctrine, a reassertion of the vanished discipline of the Church, and a statement on the 'primacy of the spiritual' in which the Church seems to hover above social and political realities without ever touching them. It was against precisely such a 'separated spirituality' – the code-word is 'angelism' – that the theologians of liberation had reacted. All these themes, it is true, were present in the teaching of Pope John Paul I. The distortion consisted not in drawing attention to them but in *reducing* his pontificate to them.

The sermon of Cardinal Pericle Felici on 6 October was a deliberate attempt to 'get behind the smile', and to show that for his intimates it was really 'a smile of suffering love':

> On the day of the solemn inauguration of his office as

Supreme Pontiff, I greeted the pope while he was still at the tomb of St Peter with the liturgical expression that 'the Lord would make him happy on earth'. Smilingly he answered: 'Yes, happy on the outside, but if only you knew what I felt like inside – *si scires*!'

Much of Felici's sermon was devoted to showing how close he had been to Pope John Paul I. In May 1978 Felici had given him what he called 'a small and very modest reproduction' of the Stations of the Cross to commemorate a retreat given to the priests and bishops of Triveneto. Moreover, the retreat which Cardinal Luciani was due to give to the priests of the diocese of Padua had in fact been given by Felici himself. He was therefore an insider, an equal, a mentor, well in on the old-boy-network that dominates the Church in Italy. Felici's interpretation of the Luciani smile as a mask of suffering was saved from caricature only by a last-gasp reference to scripture. Luciani could say with St Paul: 'I am filled with consolation and joy even in my sufferings' (2 Corinthians 7: 4).

It could be that Felici's interpretation of the smile of Pope Luciani was correct. It matched exactly Peter Nicholls' description of the peculiar character of Italian humour: 'Italians laugh from a deep sense of pessimism, of the hopelessness of the human condition. Life is basically difficult, sometimes dreadful, and one way to deal with it is to laugh. Laughing or crying will make no difference one way or another' (*Italia, Italia*, Collins, Fontana, 1973, p. 157). This was precisely the attitude displayed by Luciani when he appeared on the balcony of St Peter's on the morning after his election. His first word, '*Ieri*' ('Yesterday') got a laugh because it was accompanied by a self-deprecating shrug which said in effect, 'Why on earth should this have happened to me?' He was the little man struggling against inevitable adversity. He was Pinocchio always getting into trouble. He was – more gravely – out of his depth. His idea of being a 'pastoral' bishop of Rome was that he should visit the parish churches of Rome one by one, day by day.

It was pointed out to him that to emerge from the Vatican posed diplomatic questions of the most delicate nature and that, in any case, he would have to be accompanied by a motor-cycle escort and flashing police lights. Why can't I just walk, he asked plaintively, or get a bus? The idea of a pope on the loose was such evident nonsense (to his aides) that he went back, even more desperately, to his smile.

As always in human affairs but especially in impenetrable Vatican affairs – there was event and interpretation. And the re-interpretation of the brief pontificate was designed to prepare the public for a very different kind of pope. In retrospect the meteor flashing briefly across the sky seemed to outsiders like the transient fantasy of a Church at last reconciled, with no controverted questions and no seriously divisive issues, presided over by a genial, smiling pope who loved children, the poor and the third world. The fantasy was dangerous because it was illusory: and yet it was possible just to believe in it because Pope John Paul I's death had spared him the conflicts – on Puebla, on women priests, on inter-communion that lay just over the horizon. But there would inevitably be a rude awakening. Any successor would find it difficult to measure up to the 'image' of Pope John Paul I, and would need time to establish his own personal style. The Confalonieri-Siri-Felici re-drawing of the portrait was an attempt to forestall disappointment and to indicate the direction in which the cardinals should now be looking: towards a strong-minded pope of uncompromising doctrinal firmness. Whether he could smile or not was secondary.

Two further factors completed the 'revisionist' process. It was hinted that Pope John Paul I's *naïveté* and ignorance of world affairs had already led him into trouble. The evidence for this was meagre enough. Addressing Spanish pilgrims he had incautiously exclaimed – perhaps one of the few phrases he knew in Spanish – '*Arriba España*', evidently unaware that this was a Fascist slogan now thoroughly out of favour in democratic Spain. He also wrote a letter to the mayor of Jerusalem and addressed it in his own hand to the

State of Israel – thus conferring diplomatic recognition on Israel which the Holy See had so long withheld. He had cheerfully received General Videla, president of Argentina, without realizing that this would be badly received by Latin American Catholics who were preparing their Puebla meeting which, it was hoped, would give the military dictatorships with their 'doctrine of national security' a nasty shock. The purpose of this whispering campaign – it was no more than that – was to suggest that after a brief interlude of whimsical charm and avowed inexperience, there would be a return to the more solid virtues of experience. The cardinals had had their extravagant little holiday, God had provided, and next time round they would allow experience to count in their election of the pope.

This was all the more true in that, after the relative tranquillity of August, political considerations began to weigh upon the conclave. Rockets were crashing down upon the Maronite Christians of the Lebanon and on 6 October Cardinal Confalonieri dispatched telegrams to the Syrian President, General Assad, and to the Secretary General of the United Nations, Kurt Waldheim. The telegram to General Hafez El Assad said:

> The sacred college of cardinals assembled in the Vatican from all parts of the world is profoundly grieved at the numerous victims and grave destruction that have been caused by the bombardments and the fighting going on in the Lebanon in the last five days. We make a pressing appeal to your Excellency to facilitate an urgent truce and meanwhile to order an immediate halt to the bombings that are striking especially defenceless civilians. In expressing our confidence in the action of your Excellency, we beseech Almighty God to assist all parties involved so that through speedy and wise initiatives they may help to bring peace and security to the Lebanese people, who are living in suffering and in terror.

A similar message, of equal length, was dispatched to Kurt

Waldheim. There were more local reasons for tenseness. The Red Brigades were active again – there were two murders in the week before the conclave – and the publication of the so-called 'will' of Aldo Moro, extracted from him under torture and the fallacious promise of release, contributed to the mood of gloom. Moro said that he would have broken with the Christian Democratic Party which had proved so indifferent to his fate.

In this atmosphere, there appeared an extraordinary article in *Osservatore Romano*, written by Corrado Balducci, a Vatican demonologist. He described the future pontificate in dark, apocalyptic hues: 'During the next pontificate there will be a great cataclysm, which could take the form of a third world war.' This dire prediction was based on the fantasies of Malachy (1094–1148), Archbishop of Armagh, who had provided mottoes for all popes from the mid-twelfth century until the end of time. His last pope was called Peter II. To do St Malachy justice, most scholars believe that the series of sayings attributed to him – vague enough to be plausible whatever happens – were in fact a sixteenth century forgery. Malachy was let off the hook. Nevertheless commentators strove desperately to discover how *de medietate lunae* applied to Luciani (he had the syllable lu- in his name, and was pope between two full moons) while wondering what on earth *de labore solis* indicated about his successor. It was difficult to take this nonsense solemnly. But Balducci's predictions of troubled times ahead were to be taken seriously. They contributed to the 'strategy of tension' that was being used by right-wing elements in the Roman Curia. In a collapsing world, the papacy alone would be able to stand up to the forces of evil. Even Cardinal Ursi of Naples, considered by many to be the closest in spirit to the late pope, uttered warnings about an impending conflict between good and evil. The conclusion to this line of thinking – if it can so be called – was that the cardinals should elect someone of titanic strength who would be able to lead the Church through the dark days ahead.

And where was the candidate who could satisfy these

dramatic requirements? Cardinal Siri of Genoa was waiting quietly in the wings. Many believed that his hour had come. A quite unprecedented press campaign was mounted in his favour in the week before the conclave. Newspaper after newspaper announced that he would take into the conclave a 'packet' of some fifty votes. The state-controlled radio gave a ten-minute biography of Cardinal Siri on Thursday 12 October, as though he had already been elected pope. Despite these flattering attentions, Cardinal Siri was not at all pleased, and by the end of the week he was proclaiming himself 'the most maligned and reviled of men'. For the press campaign inevitably provoked a counter-campaign from all those who remembered Siri's actions at the Council when he had constantly sided with the minority of hard-core conservatives (including Lefebvre) who opposed liturgical reform, religious liberty, ecumenism and – above all collegiality. In the pontificate of Pius XII Siri had been a prodigy, becoming bishop in 1944 and cardinal in 1953. He was said to have been Pius's designated successor, and fought a rude battle with Roncalli in the 1958 conclave. It was as though the Church had gone into a Rip van Winkle slumber for twenty years. The year was undoubtedly 1978, but here was Siri re-living 1958.

Cardinal Siri did not like Pope John XXIII. He once said that 'it will take the Church fifty years to recover from his pontificate'. He did not like Pope Paul VI, who completed the Council, an event described by Siri as 'the greatest disaster in recent ecclesiastical history' (and by 'recent' he meant in the last five hundred years). Not surprisingly, therefore, the Council was implemented in Genoa with foot-dragging slowness. Altars did not face the people. Evening Masses were discouraged. Women in trousers were denounced. So it was not unjust of the authors of *The Inner Elite* to describe him as 'the arch-conservative's arch-conservative'. But in recent years, Siri had grown more prudent. He had taken to saying that he was above all dissenting parties in the Church, and that he was a 'centrist' or 'moderate' or, even more oddly, an 'independent'. The labels do not much matter when we can inspect the record. But it was not altogether clear whether the ostensible pro-Siri campaign was devised by his friends or his enemies. The enemies might be setting him up in order to knock him down. But on the other hand, with friends such as his, what need was there of enemies?

But in the end Siri contributed to his own undoing by first of all giving, and then saying that he had not given, an interview to *Gazzetta del Populo* in which he abused the interviewer in a most unreasonable manner, and showed himself to be distinctly lacking in that quality of 'serenity' so prized by *Osservatore Romano*. 'That's a question I would only take from my confessor,' he said at one point. 'I don't know how you could ask such a stupid question. If you really want an answer you will have to sit there and shut up for three hours.' This interview undoubtedly took place, and the casette exists to prove it. But there was a breach of journalistic ethics in that the newspaper had agreed not to publish it until Sunday 15 October, by which time the cardinals would have been incommunicado in the conclave and unable to read what their brother of Genoa had been saying. In fact the interview was published on Saturday 14 October, and with it the Siri campaign may be said to have collapsed into farce. A deadly *mot* from Cardinal König finished him off altogether. Would Cardinal Siri, if elected pope, restore the coronation ceremony? 'No,' said Cardinal König, 'he would have a simple, humble ceremony in St Peter's Square; but then afterwards, in private, he would have a marvellous coronation with all his friends present and incense billowing all over the place.'

The 'strategy of tension' was not working very well: the idea was to scare the cardinals into voting for a 'strong' (i.e. right-wing) pope who would make no concessions to 'collegiality' (which is interpreted in these circles as weakness). But the Siri followers remained loyal to him, despite the battering he had received, and he undoubtedly went into the conclave with a number of votes. According to one source there was talk of a deal between Siri and Benelli, and the telephone was undoubtedly ringing between Florence (whither Benelli had once again retired) and Genoa. But neither was prepared to give way to the other. This would eventually determine the outcome of the conclave and permit a non-Italian to emerge. Confalonieri was this time reduced to impotence, and sat on his balcony in the via della Conciliazione watching for white smoke.

Thus we reached Saturday 14 October and once more the Mass 'for electing the pope' was presided over by Cardinal Villot at the altar of the throne. This time I had a ticket which purported to admit me into the journalists' tribune, but having battled my way up the right-hand side of St Peter's, the ushers explained that the place for journalists was on the left-hand side. I gave up the unequal struggle and clambered into an anonymous tribune some three hundred feet away from the altar. I was surrounded by a posse of German and Spanish priests who, armed with binoculars, could give a professional commentary on what was happening away beyond and behind Bernini's altar. But at least there was no problem about hearing Cardinal Villot. Once more he managed to raise the spiritual level several degrees. 'Once more' – '*ancora una volta*' – were his first words as he expounded the same Gospel of St John that he had commented on seven weeks before. It was a good example of *lectio continuata* or running commentary on the texts before him. But this time he laid stress on the human responsibility of the cardinals. 'It is as men, as responsible men, that we will have to go forward to the election,' he said. Miracles or claps of thunder were not to be expected. The verse, 'You have not chosen me, I have chosen you,' he applied directly to the conclave. Human abilities should be taken into consideration, but in the end the mandate of the college of cardinals came from God's choice and not 'from the human qualities that we may or may not possess.'

The crowd was much bigger than in August. Most were interested Romans. But there were also astonished tourists – if it's Saturday, it's Rome – who clung tightly to their guides ıor fear of getting lost. Indiscriminate cheers greeted the cardinals as they processed down the nave. As they then returned individually, it was clear that some were favourites and that others were content to be – and hoped to remain – merely voters. Cardinal Wyszinski got a great cheer as a representative of the Church of Silence, while Cardinal Benelli shook hands with all and sundry, including the Editor of *The Catholic Herald*, Richard Dowden, who noted the vigorous grip, the calloused hands and the unresponsive eyes. Cardinal Siri, already a loser, was smiling vaguely, and Cardinal Karol Wojtyla was not sufficiently well-known to be noticed. It is fair to say that the 111 cardinals looked rather more strained than they had in August. It was unreasonable to expect them to pull off another surprise in the Holy Spirit. Or so it seemed.

The October Conclave

I would like to tell you everything. It would thrill you. But I can't.

> Cardinal John J. Carberry, press
> conference, 17 October 1978

Of all the activities devised by human beings which have no economic or other necessity, and are therefore the basis of civilization, that of watching for smoke-signals from the rather undistinguished flue on the top of the Sistine Chapel is perhaps the most frustrating. Yet on the first day of the conclave a vast and expectant crowd gathered in St Peter's Square to witness the event. The morning crowd was less knowing, less professional: after all, the pundits had declared that it was impossible that there should be white smoke after only two ballots. But the crowd was in a holiday mood. There were many children with the helium filled balloons that are all the rage in Rome. Occasionally one of them would soar away into space, accompanied by cheerful cries. Copies of *Osservatore Romano*, with photographs of all 111 cardinals, were folded into improvised hats against the sun that was beating fiercely down. The most determined smoke-watchers had brought along camp-stoves and cooked lunch while they waited. But the pundits had been right, for once. The smoke which emerged at 11.26 was undoubtedly intended to be black. Vatican Radio assured its listeners that it was the first sixty seconds (others said the first thirty seconds) of smoke that counted. I made my way to the fifth-floor flat of a Polish lady, long resident in Rome, for a 'post-black-smoke' party given by Jerzy Turowicz, Editor for over thirty years of *Tygodnik Powszechny*, the Catholic paper published in Krakow.

In the evening, as darkness fell, the connoisseurs appeared, hoping for the swift harmonious surprise of the previous conclave. At 5.30 p.m. a vast searchlight beamed out from the top of the Gianiculum and fell upon the cornice of St Peter's and the stove-pipe. Now and then a pigeon would get caught in its light and pause, astonished at this new star that had appeared in the heavens. In the left-hand arm of Bernini's colonnade an improvised radio studio had been set up; TV people were on top of the colonnade. RAI – the Italian radio and TV company – had done a good job. Alleged experts (like myself) sat with ear-phones on, waiting for something to happen. There was sudden excitement as more smoke appeared at 6.40. It was an uncertain grey. A babel of commentators tossed aside their cigarettes and cried, 'It's white, no it's black, dammit.' The disappointed crowd drifted away once more. The August miracle was not going to be repeated. Even the most hard-boiled, though, had to admit that the Square looked magnificent in the television lights which seem to soften the colour of the marble, brick and stone and pick out the 140 saints like eerie giants.

Back we all trooped the next day, already knowing that this conclave was not going to be easy. The words of Cardinal Hume the previous Wednesday came to mind. Preaching on the story of the apostles caught during a storm at sea, he had said: 'There is sweat involved in the effort; and an extra pulling on the oars to make headway.' Would there be, so to speak, blood on the fawn-coloured carpet of the Sistine Chapel? The crowd was less numerous on Monday. It was a working day. To fill in the time of waiting, Vatican Radio informed its listeners that the average length of conclaves in the twentieth century was three days. 1922 had been particularly arduous: it lasted seven days. Those of a sadistic turn of mind recalled that the 1830 conclave had lasted longer than 50· days and needed more than 100 ballots to get a result. Vatican Radio, by now rather desperate, began to consult what are known in the trade as vox pops – the ordinary people in St Peter's Square. To a man (and a woman), whether they came from Nigeria or Chicago, they declared that they wanted a pope who would be like John Paul I. An English priest said that he would be disappointed if the new pope were not a man of great holiness and simplicity. But, he added cautiously, it would be a help if he had some administrative experience as well.

Meanwhile, back in the braccio of the colonnade the broadcasters waited and swopped information. Hypotheses were checked. If Cardinal Felici did not appear on the balcony, then we would immediately know that he had been elected pope (a most improbable happening). His deputy, Cardinal Oddi, was famous for his collection of pectoral crosses, but in the photographs provided by *Osservatore Romano*, which took decades off most of the cardinals, Oddi appeared indistinguishable from Felici. These were, as it turned out, vain worries. Much more serious was the fact that there were in the conclave no less than ten Johns (including Juan, Jan, Giovanni and Jean) so that if Felici announced the name *Johannem*, that would not necessarily mean that Benelli had been elected, though the crowd would undoubtedly chant out his name. Thus was the time tensely passed until at 6.19 p.m. there was a roar from the crowd. The smoke was unquestionably white and it continued to pour out for a few minutes. We had a pope, after what was assumed to be eight ballots. But who on earth was he? And – grave question for all the commentators – would they know anything about him?

At 6.44 Cardinal Felici appeared on the central balcony of St Peter's and made the announcement with his usual relish and faintly ironical smile. In full it read: '*Annuncio vobis gaudium magnum. Habemus papam, eminentissimum ac reverendissimum Dominum Carolum, sanctae Romanae ecclesiae cardinalem Wojtyla, qui sibi nomen imposuit Joannem Paulum Secundum.*' There was great enthusiasm at this wholly unexpected news. There were tears of joy. People shook hands and embraced each other.

In Warsaw that same Monday evening, 16 October, Mr Kazimierz Kakol was presiding over a press conference on the theme of the conclave. He is the minister responsible for church affairs in Poland. Communist governments consider religion so important that a special ministry is needed to keep it under control. Kakol was explaining that the choice of a new pope was a matter of some interest for Poland, since it would determine whether or not the *Ostpolitik* of Pope Paul VI would be continued. In a humorous aside he remarked that if the next pope happened to be Polish – laughter greeted this unthinkable suggestion – he would buy champagne for everyone present. Ten minutes later came the news that there was a pope and half an hour later that it was the Archbishop of Krakow, Cardinal Karol Wojtyla. Kakol turned pale, and honourably ordered the champagne. Not so very long after this, champagne corks were also popping in the Sala Borgia of the Vatican where the new pope, humbly seated in the place he had occupied at meals throughout the conclave, was toasted by his fellow cardinals.

But before that, at 7.22, Cardinal Wojtyla, now Pope John Paul II, appeared on the balcony and delighted the Roman crowd. Italians have always had great affection for Poland, as a nation that has known such intense suffering. Pope John Paul II could merely have given his blessing *urbi et orbi* in Latin. That was the tradition. But he decided to say a few words in his plain, easily intelligible Italian. He said:

Praise be Jesus Christ! (To which the crowd responded 'Now and forever'.)

Dear brothers and sisters, we are all still saddened at the death of our beloved Pope John Paul I and so the cardinals have called for a new bishop of Rome. They called him from a far-distant country – far and yet always close because of our communion in faith and Christian traditions. I was afraid to accept that responsibility, yet I do so in a spirit of obedience to the Lord and total faithfulness to Mary, our Most Holy Mother. I am speaking to you in your – no, our Italian language. If I make a mistake, please correct me. I would like to invite you to join me in professing our faith, our hope and our fidelity to Mary, the Mother of Christ and of the Church, and also to begin again on the road of history and of the Church. I begin with the help of God and the help of men.

Though without the quicksilver wit and perfect timing of Pope John Paul I, these words, delivered firmly in a voice that suggested great strength, went to the heart of the Roman crowd. He had defined himself as Bishop of Rome. He spoke first of 'your language' and then corrected himself, to 'our language'. His double reference to Mary was not objectionable to Romans. Other phrases would become more significant in retrospect as one got used to his style (the reference to the 'journey' or 'road', the insistence on 'the help of *men*'). But this was not a time for analysis. Applause was prolonged, and the 200,000 people left the Square in a state of high excitement, eagerly discussing the totally surprising turn of events.

For there was no doubt that, once again, the College of Cardinals had pulled off a surprise, not only by electing the first non-Italian pope for 455 years, but in choosing someone who was young by papal standards – only 58 – and who came from a communist country. Even before detailed interpretation could begin, it was clear that the cardinals had displayed a courage and imagination of no mean order. But how had they reached their decision? After the indiscretions of August, Cardinal Villot had exhorted them to complete secrecy, and lips were more tightly sealed. The enquiring observer was rather in the position of an intelligence officer who has to interrogate captured troops determined to give away nothing more than their name and number. So I cannot – nor can anyone else – tell you what happened in the conclave. What follows moves from a single nugget of fact and then moves on to reasonable supposition.

The only solid fact is that the conclave elected Cardinal Wojtyla after a number of ballots (which may have been eight). The smoke signals, if the rules were followed, certainly indicated eight ballots. But some of them could have been a sop to the waiting crowd. It is a fact that the cardinals showed an extreme reluctance to commit themselves on the precise number of ballots. Cardinal Roy of Quebec, with whom I shared a radio studio for CBC three days later, was asked how he felt after the eighth ballot. 'After the *last* ballot,' he cautiously began, 'I felt very relieved.' Cardinal Hume was equally wary. I asked him what conclusions could be drawn from the fact that there were this time eight ballots compared with the four (or three) of August. 'If there were eight ballots', he replied with a smile of great charm, 'then there must have been twice as many as last time.' Curiouser and curiouser, as Alice said. The number of ballots is not important in itself. But if, as some suspected, Cardinal Wojtyla had asked for some time to think and pray, and perhaps also asked for a confirming ballot, this diffidence on the exact number of ballots would be explained.

The interviews with the cardinals as they emerged from the Vatican provided a few further clues. No one claimed that there had been the virtual unanimity asserted in August. There was much less talk about the Holy Spirit – not that he was felt to have been absent, but there was a keener sense that he works through human agencies. The outline of what had happened was given by Cardinal Avelar Brandão Vilela from Brazil (who has, according to *The Inner Elite*, 'a princely life-style'). He said that they had failed to find a consensus around any of the Italian cardinals and, to resolve the impasse, had been obliged to look for a non-Italian. This was supported by Cardinal Benelli. He was looking rather tired, had lost his suitcase, and was somewhat testy with Italian journalists who asked him stupid questions ('Is this a significant event?' 'Of course it is a significant event'). But he was more forthcoming in an interview the next day in *Gazzetta del Populo* when he said: 'There was

not the convergence of votes on an Italian needed to be
elected pope. But this did not matter, for in the Church
there are no foreigners.' True enough, but this glossed over
the novelty of the event. Pope John Paul II himself, in his
speech to the cardinals in the consistorial hall on Wednesday
18 October, recognized that they had done something surprising that required explanation: 'Venerable brothers, it
was an act of trust and at the same time an act of great
courage to have wished to elect a "non-Italian" pope as
Bishop of Rome. I can't say more about this, except to
accept the decision of the College of Cardinals.' Thus, from
the most authoritative source, we learn that the departure
from precedent required courage and that, therefore, it was
not a step easily taken.

Cardinal Wojtyla was not the man they had in mind at
the start of the conclave. The witness of Brandão Vilela and
Benelli is that a non-Italian was considered only after the
Italian candidates had been tried and had failed to gain the
75 votes needed. Fabrizio De Santis in *Corriere della Sera*,
19 October 1978, claimed to know that in the early ballots
Poletti, Ursi, Felice and Colombo each gained some 20–30
votes, and that with none of them making any significant
headway, they were gradually abandoned. The Italian
cardinals, in other words, had cancelled each other out.
There are two objections to the De Santis speculation. First,
it does not suggest the 'thrilling story' that Cardinal John
J. Carberry would like to have told, and secondly, it
ignores completely the roles of Siri and Benelli.

Another 'scenario' is possible which takes account of these
objections. Though Siri had discredited himself in the eyes
of the public, it was difficult to believe that he did not have
some significant support from the 25 cardinals who had
voted for him in August; and they may have been joined
by a few cardinals who were impressed by the doom-laden
considerations on the need for a 'strong pope'. As for
Benelli, he now matched the job specification well. Whereas
in August he was the behind-the-scenes pope-maker rather
than a candidate, the situation had now changed utterly.

After the sudden death of the pope and in view of the intolerable demands of the office, a younger man – someone in his fifties – could now be contemplated with equanimity and relief. Then there was the fact that the inexperience of Luciani had led him into mistakes, and one could conclude that this time experience would count. But in that case Benelli would be a strong contender, for no one could equal him in experience. He had been in the thick of things since he became *sostituto* in 1967. He had handled all the dossiers. He had been the hour-glass connecting the pope with the Church. He had, moreover, gained enough 'pastoral experience' in Florence not to be ruled out on the grounds that he was exclusively a bureaucrat. He had travelled extensively and made important speeches. He had a modern 'image' and had not been disgraced when he appeared at the U.S. Eucharistic Congress in Philadelphia in 1976 alongside the two great folk-heroes of contemporary Catholicism – Mother Teresa and Dom Helder Camara. He could undoubtedly be described as a 'strong man' – his efficiency was legendary and rather alarming – but he was at the same time committed to the theology of Vatican II.

That would have been the point at issue in a Siri–Benelli contest. One suggestion is that Benelli reached 70 or so votes and came within an ace of being elected, but that he was constantly opposed by about forty cardinals coming from opposite ends of the spectrum. The Siri group would continue to veto him, while some of the progressives, knowing his authoritarian ways, would in no circumstances vote for him. I prefer not to name the curialist who said that 'a Benelli papacy would mean twenty years of dictatorship'. The quality called 'spirituality', and which Cardinals like Dearden of Detroit said could be felt instinctively, was not his strong suit. He seemed to some more like a manager in Church Inc. than a man of God. But Benelli is also a *bon prince*, and now that a candidate in his fifties had been seriously considered, and that the Italians had effectively destroyed each other, the way was open for the leading non-Italian. The imaginative leap could be made.

Indeed, it had already been made by a number of cardinals. For Cardinal Wojtyla was well-known and popular. He was in fact much better known than Cardinal Luciani. According to Cardinal Confalonieri, he had received a certain number of votes in the August conclave. Despite his comparative youthfulness   which now seemed a positive advantage – he had taken part in all four sessions of the Second Vatican Council (unlike Benelli). And he had been present at all five meetings of the Synod between 1967 and 1977. In 1971 he had been elected a member of the Secretariat of the Synod, and in 1974 had presented an important theological report on evangelization. Those who had sat with him on the congregations for the Sacraments, for Divine Worship, for the Clergy and Catholic Education, valued him as a patient listener who could sum up positions with clarity and fair-mindedness. His intellectual stature was not in doubt. His grasp of languages was another positive factor. He was quite plainly wedded to the Council and there could be no question about his strength of character: anyone who had to deal with the Polish authorities for twenty years would have to be robust, patient, clearheaded and subtle. Moreover – and this was decisive in his election – though he had stressed the importance of the local church and was intensely proud of his own ancient diocese of Krakow, he had never thought in terms of opposition between the local church and the Roman Curia. In 1976 Pope Paul VI paid him the honour of inviting him to preach the Lenten retreat for himself and the Curia. This task was usually entrusted to a Franciscan or some other Roman member of a religious order. By this retreat, which was later published under the title *Segno di Contraddizione* (Vita e Pensiero, Catholic University of Milan, 1977), he became known to the Curia and the Curia liked what it saw.

Such post-factum rationalizations do not, of course, mean that the election was inevitable; but they do help to make it intelligible. The reason that almost all observers missed Cardinal Wojtyla was that they simply underestimated the courage and imagination of the College of Cardinals. It was wrongly thought that they *could not* elect a pope from Eastern Europe because of the incalculable political consequences of such a choice. But they took that risk, seized the initiative, and in the immediate, had the Polish government floundering. One of the astutest brains in the conclave was that of Cardinal König of Vienna. He knows Eastern Europe well, having been charged with various missions (which he always insists are pastoral rather than diplomatic). Vienna has an historic relationship with the whole of the Danube region, and the southern part of Poland, including Krakow, was part of the Austro-Hungarian Empire from the end of the eighteenth century until after the First World War. Moreover, we know that Cardinal König had always said quite openly that the time had come to consider a non-Italian as pope. It was clear that he had Cardinal Wojtyla on his short list.

So had the group of four Latin American and Spanish cardinals, including Juan Landazuri Ricketts of Peru, who bought copies of *Segno di Contraddizione* on their arrival in Rome for the funeral of Pope John Paul I. To read a man's book is the simplest way to find out what he is like. One also recalled that Cardinal Joseph Ratzinger of Munich had warned, before the conclave and rather superfluously, against 'Italian left-wing pressures' on the College of Cardinals: Wojtyla's intelligent, non-bigoted opposition to communism would commend him to the German cardinals with whom the Poles had just been publicly reconciled, thanks to Cardinal Wyszinski's visit to West Germany, when he said Mass in the concentration camp of Dachau. The Wojtyla constituency was building up. One should also add that the U.S. cardinals, and especially Cardinal Krol who is of Polish origin, had been cultivating good relations with the Polish bishops and had been on spectacular visits to Czestochowa. But even Cardinal Krol admitted that the result was a surprise. He said rather cryptically: 'If one or other of you did not guess what would happen, then you have a lot of company; we have again witnessed the presence and activity of the Holy Spirit.'

It was Cardinal Krol, too, who painted a touching picture of Cardinal Wojtyla just after his election, seated alone at the table beneath Michelangelo's 'Last Judgement', his head in his hands, his body slumped – the loneliness of the long-distance pope. It was this hint which gave rise to the unsubstantiated story that Cardinal Wojtyla had asked for time to pray before accepting the papal office. But the pathos of the papacy was a theme stressed by Cardinal Hume on the day after the election. Asked how he had reacted, he said: 'I felt desperately sad for the man. But somebody has to carry this tremendous burden, and be confined in this small area. There comes a time when all the clapping stops, when the pope ceases to be news, and that is when the truth dawns.' But he added that Pope John Paul II had the toughness to cope. His strength is rooted in his Polish background and the tradition of his people. To that background we must now turn.

12

The Wojtyla Story

> The Church has led you here to lift from you by sacramental grace the chains of your personal slavery. Once you have a taste for this freedom, then the desire is awakened for other freedoms, social and civic. We do not defend ourselves against the charge that the Church is a rebel.
>
> Cardinal Stefan Wyszinski, quoted in Lucien Blit, *The Eastern Pretender*, London 1965, p. 217

Krakow, says the official guide book, 'is a gem among European towns'. No one who has visited the place would quarrel with that judgement. By some miracle it has survived invasion, occupation and the tramp of armed men. While Warsaw was systematically devastated so that 95 per cent of its buildings were in ruins by the end of the war, sleepy old Krakow, outside the main battle lines, escaped destruction, both in 1939 when the Germans occupied Poland, and in 1945 when the Red Army 'liberated' the city. Krakow owes its origin to its position on the River Vistula and especially to the limestone rock of Wawel Hill on which stands the Castle of Wawel, residence and burial place of Polish kings until 1609. The cathedral forms part of the complex of buildings that make up the castle. The wrought-iron monogram K beneath a crown commemorates King Kasimir the Great, the last king of the Piast dynasty in the fourteenth century. Nestling in the shadow of the castle is the city proper, with its Renaissance market place (the *Rynek Glowny*) and the church of St Mary in the top right-hand corner. St Mary's boasts Wit Stwosz's five-hundred-year old carved altar piece, and on the hour a trumpeter appears in its tower to mark the time. His trumpet call is always unfinished in memory of a trumpeter long ago who was killed, in full blast, by a Tartar arrow.

Krakow is a civilized place which still has a flavour of the elegant café society of the Austro-Hungarian Empire to which it belonged in the nineteenth century. Despite communism, it still has eight full-time professional theatres, and cabarets in which the art of satire, though circumscribed, is not altogether dead. On my first visit to Krakow in 1967 – still in the dark days of Gomulka – I went to the famous restaurant Wierzynek where once the Kings of Poland, Bohemia and Hungary were entertained by a rich city merchant. A painting recalls their meeting, and the menu explains that although kings are no more and the guests are no longer served on plates of gold, the management would nevertheless like to treat them 'as though they were kings'. As I made my way into the restaurant with an English friend, our interpreter, and a Polish Jesuit who had come down from Zakopane in the Tatra Mountains to listen to my lecture, a black student tried to stop the priest, who had no business, he claimed, to be entering a socialist restaurant. The waiters immobilized the student, welcomed the Jesuit, placed a bottle of wodka and a Union Jack on the table, and the three-piece orchestra gave a tolerable rendering of 'Colonel Bogey' in honour of the British guests.

Karol Wojtyla was not born in Krakow, though it became his spiritual home. He was born 30 kilometres away in the market town of Wadowice on 18 May 1920. His life-span covers, more or less, that of independent Poland. Wadowice before the war was a place of some 10,000 inhabitants, a centre for the sale of wheat, potatoes and beetroot, the local agricultural produce. The baroque church with its onion domes still survives, and the house where Karol was born is already a place of pilgrimage. Wadowice was also a garrison town, and Karol's father, a full-time soldier, was stationed there. Surviving photographs show a rather severe, balding man in pince-nez, with a neat moustache, alongside his sailor-suited younger son. His uniform reveals that he was what was called 'an administrative officer', a category that was abolished after 1926. He was widowed in 1923 and Karol's elder brother, the first of the family to receive a proper education, became a doctor and died before the war of an infection caught in the hospital where he worked. The writings of Wojtyla are not strong on autobiographical detail, but one does gather that he had to pinch and scrape to get through his gymnasium studies in Wadowice. In 1938 he moved to Krakow to begin the study of Polish literature at the celebrated Jagiellonian University, founded in 1364 by King Kasimir the Great and later supported by the Queen of Poland, Jadwiga, who was beatified only in the twentieth century. In its early years nearly half the university population came from abroad. Its most famous students were the astronomer Nicolaus Copernicus and the original of the notorious Dr Faustus. Communist party members also point out that from 1912 to 1914, Vladimir Lenin, who was later to make a name for himself, used to come and read in the University's well-stocked library.

But in 1938–39 the Jagiellonian University was a place where Polish culture flourished. Doom and destruction lay just round the corner, but it was still possible to dream of a renaissance of Polish literature. Wojtyla shared in these aspirations. He tried his hand at poetry. He joined a troupe of actors known as the *Teatr Rapsodyczny* or 'Rhapsodic Theatre'. The founder and director of this theatre was Mieczyslaw Kotlarczyk, who is still alive and active. The theatre survived the war, but fell foul of the authorities during the Stalinist era, and was abolished. When, a few years ago, Kotlarczyk published in Italy *The Art of the Word* in which he expounded his theories, the preface was written by Cardinal Wojtyla. Kotlarczyk's theatre was based on poetic declamation. It had affinities with romantic drama, was concerned with heroic exploits, mostly from the Polish Middle Ages, and got the reputation of being *avant-garde* – no doubt because the verse dramas were sometimes played in modern dress.

When the war came and sudden, devastating defeat, all cultural life came to a stop. The country had been cynically carved up between the Germans and the Russians – an event which satisfied Evelyn Waugh or at least his character, Guy Crouchback, since now 'the enemy was at last plain in view, huge and hateful, all disguise cast off'. The Germans who occupied Krakow were particularly keen to stamp out all signs of intellectual life, since the Poles were regarded as an inferior, non-Aryan, slave race. In June 1940 the professors and teachers in the University were summoned to a meeting, ostensibly to discuss its re-opening. Only those who were wise enough to stay away escaped death or the concentration camp. Karol's father died in 1941 so that he was an orphan of twenty-one in the darkest days of the war. The only way to stay alive at that time was to have an *Arbeitskarte* or work-permit. Without a work-permit one would be rounded up and deported to slave-labour camps in Germany or elsewhere. Wojtyla, after a spell in a stone quarry, accordingly went to work in the Solvay chemical factory, a Belgian-owned company, which still survives under different management. But the 'Rhapsodic Theatre' continued in clandestinity. The survivors of the troupe performed in private apartments before invited audiences of twenty to thirty people. Wojtyla belonged, therefore, to the 'cultural resistance movement' rather than the Home Army. This prefigured his opposition to the communists: it was important to keep alive the spirit and traditions of Poland, whoever the rulers of the country might happen to be.

But in 1942 Wojtyla disappeared from the Solvay factory and was not heard of or seen again until after the war. Various fantastic explanations have been proposed to fill this gap: it was alleged that he had married and been widowed. This story is unfortunately false and the truth is much simpler. The Faculty of Theology had been abolished along with the rest of the University, and the three seminaries of Krakow had likewise been suppressed. But Cardinal Adam Sapieha, Archbishop of Krakow, had decided to welcome a few theological students into his episcopal palace, a roomy early nineteenth-century building on Franciszkańska Street. Once inside, Wojtyla and his four companions could not think of emerging, for they were now without papers and would have been arrested straight away. They must have felt rather nervous when the notorious Hans Frank, head of the German administration in occupied Poland, visited the cardinal. Sapieha would pointedly invite him to share the corn coffee, beetroot jam and black bread that were all the Poles had to eat. Sapieha, who was known as Prince-Prince Sapieha (he was a prince by birth and a 'prince of the Church'), was a man of considerable personality. The Primate of Poland, Hlond, had fled to France, where he remained for the duration of the war, but Sapieha stayed behind to share in the fate of his people.

Wojtyla was ordained on 1 November 1946. Few priests can have had a more unconventional preparation for ordination. And it needed considerable courage to be ordained at a time when the future of the country and the Church were so hazardous. The frontiers of Poland had been shifted westwards: vast tracts of land were lost to the Russians, while the Poles regained – after 600 years – some of the shattered cities of Germany. The Russian-backed communist regime was imposed on a reluctant nation: this was not the sort of liberation for which the resistance movements had fought so bitterly. Yet a direct and immediate onslaught on the Church was not expected, for in Poland, whatever might be true in Hungary or Yugoslavia, it was impossible to drive a wedge between the Church and the nation: the Church had suffered with the nation, kept alive its spirit of resistance, and two thousand priests had been executed or had died in concentration camps.

Wojtyla's talents had been recognized and he was sent abroad for further studies. At the Angelicum University in Rome (1946–48) he wrote a dissertation on 'The Concept of Faith in the Writings of St John of the Cross'. It was interesting that he should have been drawn to the Spanish mystical poet for whom faith appears as a series of paradoxes, a darkness that illuminates, a music that is soundless. To someone coming from war-ravaged Poland, the idea that God is reached by the *via negativa*, by emptying the mind of all distracting images, must have seemed congenial if austere. The director of the dissertation was Père Réginald Garrigou-Lagrange, a French Dominican whose Thomism was unrelenting and who saw in St John of the Cross a confirmation of the main theses of Aquinas. But the stay in Rome meant that Wojtyla now had a good command of Italian, and during his summer vacations he worked among the Polish exiles in the Pas de Calais and in Belgium, and thus picked up a knowledge of French as well.

On his return to Krakow in 1948 he became curate at Niegowié and a year later at St Florian's Church in the heart of Krakow. He continued his studies and in 1951 was given a sabbatical year from parish duties so that he could begin his 'teaching' thesis at the Catholic University of Lublin (KUL), the only independent university between the Elbe and the Pacific. His subject was 'On the Possibility of Basing a Catholic Ethics on the System of Max Scheler'. Scheler (1874–1928) was another significant choice. He was a Catholic philosopher formed in the phenomenological method developed by Husserl. His starting-point was the irreducible uniqueness of human and humanizing emotions. Love, for instance, could not be reduced to a mere biological instinct or a cry for help or the Id. The notion of love was central in Scheler. It is, as he wrote, 'the pioneer of values', that is to say, the way by which goodness and other values are discerned and discovered. Unless we love, we cannot claim to know. This was in fact the revival of a theme dear to St Augustine. Scheler, finally, laid great stress on the importance of 'models' in the development of the moral life: unless we have heroes or, better, saints, to look up to and emulate, the moral life will remain flabby and undirected. All these ideas remained a part of Wojtyla's mental outlook and can be traced in his later writings such as *Person and Acts* and especially *Love and Responsibility* (first published in Polish in 1960), in which he defended the anti-contraception tradition of the Church, but expressed it in terms of person rather than nature. *Love and Responsibility* may be said to have anticipated *Humanae Vitae*.

By now Wojtyla was professor of moral philosophy at the Catholic University of Lublin and was also teaching in the Krakow seminary (the Faculty of Theology had not been re-opened after the war, and this remained a sore point with Wojtyla, especially when the government-sponsored Academy of Catholic Theology – AKT – was opened in Warsaw). Relations between Church and state had deteriorated in the Stalinist period. In 1948 Catholic Action and other Church organizations were declared illegal. In 1950 Cardinal Sapieha and the newly appointed Archbishop of Warsaw, Stefan Wyszinski, wrote to President Bodeslaw Bierut, who was also First Secretary of the Party, to complain that the government had been guilty of bad faith in its dealings with the Church. The government replied by accusing the bishops of hostility to the People's Republic. On 14 April 1950 three representatives of the hierarchy met three communists and signed a document which acknowledged the pope as supreme head of the Church in all matters relating to faith and church order, while the bishops said that they recognized the recovered western territories as an integral part of Poland and undertook to ask the pope to appoint residential bishops there. Cardinal Sapieha made a special visit to Rome but was unable to persuade Pope Pius XII to accept this compromise. Much later, Cardinal Wyszinski, who also had his difficulties with Pius XII, complained bitterly at a press conference in Rome: 'You speak of the Church of Silence, but here in Rome is the Church of the deaf.' This sense of being misunderstood by Rome partly accounts for the mistrust of the Vatican's *Ostpolitik*.

But there is a danger of getting bogged down in the complicated story of Church-state relations in Poland which, as Neal Ascherson said, 'are the Pripet Marshes of contemporary history'. As a young priest, Wojtyla was not involved in these top-level negotiations. They were happening elsewhere and were conducted by others. One indication of his attitude of 'inner emigration' is provided by the fact that he wrote a great deal of poetry at this period. It was published in *Znak*, the monthly magazine belonging to the Movement of Catholic Intellectuals, or in *Tygodnik Powszechny*, its weekly paper. The editor of *Tygodnik Powszechny*, then as now Jerzy Turowicz, told me that Wojtyla's poems were accepted on merit, and not because they were written by a priest. 'We reject,' he said rather grandly, 'ninety per cent of the poetry we receive.' Wojtyla's poems were long, written in a rather craggy free verse form, and dealt with philosophical and moral themes. They were certainly not merely the pious elucubrations of a young and introverted priest, and they were not always religious. They announce that fundamental Christian humanism from which Wojtyla has never departed. It came out in his closing remark at the inauguration Mass: 'And I also appeal to all men – to every man (and with what veneration the apostle of Christ must utter this word "man").' And one of the major themes of his retreat for the Roman Curia was a meditation on the words of St Irenaeus: 'The glory of God is that man should be fully alive.'

Writing poetry, if nothing else, supposes sensitivity to language and to feelings. But Wojtyla may have wondered how it fitted in with his priestly ministry. (He might have remembered Gerard Manley Hopkins, whose poems wrought more than ever his rather eccentric sermons did.) In any event, he never signed his poems in *Znak* and *Tygodnik Powszechny* and used instead the pseudonym of Andrzej Jawień. This was the name of the hero of a famous pre-war novel, *The Sky in Flames*, written by Jan Parandowski. The dramatic title refers not to the horror of war but to the young hero's loss of Christian faith. (In a subsequent, post-war volume Jawień recovered his faith.) Why Wojtyla chose this pseudonym we do not know, but it may contain a hint that faith for him is valueless unless it has been tested and tried. He is not a man for the easy option.

Nor were there any easy options for the Polish Church in the early 1950s. In September 1953 Wyszinski, who had been made a cardinal earlier in the year, was placed under house arrest (he was in fact confined to a monastery), and by the end of the year eight bishops and 900 priests had been arrested. By the year 1955 there were over 2,000 bishops, priests and Catholic laymen in prison. There was no darker time. But then, with the death of Stalin and Khrushchev's denunciations of his crimes at the Twentieth Party Congress, it became possible to hope again. In 1956 Gomulka came to power, promised that 'the Polish road to socialism' would be followed, released the imprisoned Catholics and re-instated Wyszinski as Primate. It was the Polish 'spring'. There was optimism in the air. Communism could be humanized after all. Philosophers like Adam Schaff and Leszek Kolakowski were trying to rescue Marxism from Stalinism by a return to the younger Marx and by remaining in dialogue with existentialist philosophers. The optimism was short-lived and the hopes unfulfilled, but there would henceforth be no return to the overt persecution of the Stalinist era. From now on conflict would take the form of continual harassment over a long – indeed endless – period. The battle was on for the 'soul' and the youth of the nation. According to the official ideology, Poland was a model socialist country in which the 'new man' was being shaped, free from the alienations of capitalism. According to the Church, Poland was a bastion of Christianity and therefore liberty, placed strategically in the heart of Central Europe. There were two versions of history.

In 1958 Wojtyla was appointed Auxiliary Bishop of Krakow. At 38, he was the youngest member of the episcopacy. On 13 January 1964 he became Archbishop. He had been living in a small two-roomed flat and hoped to be able to stay there when he became Archbishop. But the Vicar General thought it was undignified for him to live in such a poky place and that he ought to move into the palace. Wojtyla held out for four weeks, and then moved into the residence where he had spent, in hiding, those wartime years.

13

Archbishop of Krakow

*If we cannot destroy the Church, at least let us stop it
from causing harm.*

An anonymous Polish communist, quoted
in a Samizdat publication

Karol Wojtyla was only 43 when he was appointed Archbishop of Krakow in 1964. He was well-known locally for
his theological teaching and writing and for his work among
students. But he had already moved onto the wider international scene. By 1964 there had been two sessions of
Vatican Council II, and Wojtyla had been present at both
of them (though it was touch and go whether he would be
granted a passport for the opening session in 1962). He had
spoken in the aula on 7 November 1962 on liturgy, and
on 21 November 1962 on the sources of relevation. Among
the other speakers on the second occasion were Cardinal
François Marty of Paris and Bishop Christopher Butler
O.S.B. Wojtyla was not overawed by the company he was
keeping. Bishop-theologians are rarer than one might think,
and his contributions were listened to with interest. On
23 September 1963 he urged that the Church should be seen
as 'People of God' before there was any treatment of the
hierarchy, on the grounds that the whole should come before
the part. The implications of this for the theology of the laity
were considerable; and this speech (they were known as
interventions) showed that Wojtyla was on the side of those
who favoured a more biblical and less clerical approach to
the Church. Those who misguidedly supposed that all Polish
theology was a defence of sturdy peasant piety or that all

Polish bishops were as traditionalist as Cardinal Wyszinski, were pleasantly surprised.

In later interventions at the Council Wojtyla made use of his experience under a communist regime to enrich the debates. There was one dangerous moment when the very existence of the declaration of religious liberty was threatened by attacks from conservatives who thought that it conceded too much to 'error', and it was Wojtyla who pointed out that the draft document contained both a concession and a claim. The Church could only claim religious liberty in the face of a hostile government if it were prepared to concede it where it was strong. For that reason, the declaration would be a great help to the Catholics of Eastern Europe in their struggles with their governments. One recalls how anguished Luciani had been over the question of religious liberty; Wojtyla was not at all anguished.

His first-hand experience of atheism was also appreciated. He rejected an out-and-out condemnation, since that would make subsequent dialogue impossible. He preferred the 'heuristic' approach which tried to find common ground with unbelievers. One had to begin where people were, in the thick of human experience, and move on from there. A 'pastoral' treatment of atheism   or rather of atheists, since atheism as such did not exist   would have to adopt this method. He concluded: 'It is not the role of the Church to lecture unbelievers. We are involved in a search along with our fellow men . . . Let us avoid moralizing or the suggestion that we have a monopoly of the truth. One of the major defects of this draft is that in it the Church appears merely as an authoritarian institution' (21 October 1963).

Archbishop Wojtyla was a member of the Mixed Commission which had to deal with 'Schema 13', an early version of what eventually became *The Church in the World of Today*. One of the major battles on this text – in retrospect it may seem rather futile – concerned the title to be given to it. It could not be called a 'constitution', some argued, because it was not merely concerned with principles but with their practical application. There survives the record of an exchange between members of the commission in which Bishop Butler suggested, quite rightly, that those who wanted to change the title really wanted to downgrade the document. But it was Wojtyla who suggested the compromise that eventually won the day: 'The document really is a "constitution" but one that is "pastoral". The latter term should be carefully explained: it is much more concerned with life than with doctrine. Moreover, Part I is also very pastoral in places, especially where it discussed the human person. Both parts must be seen in a pastoral light' (cf. *The Fouth Session*, Xavier Rynne, Farrer, Strauss and Giroux Inc., 1965; Faber and Faber, 1966). Thus *The Church in the World of Today*, often known by its first words, *Gaudium et Spes*, became and will remain for all time a 'pastoral constitution'.

Back in Krakow after the end of the Council in December 1965, Archbishop Wojtyla was caught up in the preparations for the celebration of a thousand years of Polish Christianity, which came in 1966. It was the brainchild of Cardinal Wyszinski. While exiled in a monastery in Eastern Poland in the Stalinist era, he had re-read Henryk Sienkiewicz's historical novel *Potop* (*The Flood*) which recounted Poland's famous victory over the Swedish invaders in 1655. On the eve of the decisive battle King John Kasimir took a vow on behalf of the nation to serve God and Our Lady, to rid the country of foreign invaders and to improve the social conditions of the Polish people. Wyszinski's ingenious idea was that the same vow, suitably adapted, should be made by the Polish people during the millennium celebrations of 1966. This had been prepared in depth, with an educational programme lasting ten years. The Bishops gave a lead by taking the vow at Czestochowa in August 1956, and year by year sermons and catechesis developed a course of instruction designed to make all Catholics aware of their responsibilities. It was an act of outright defiance of the government. For by repeating that Our Lady was 'Queen of Poland' the bishops were not merely uttering a pious formula: they were declaring that she was the true sovereign of Poland and that, therefore, the current rulers of the country were temporary usurpers.

The government responded by doing everything in its power to obstruct the celebrations. Football matches were re-arranged to coincide with special Masses. Children were taken away on excursions to prevent them attending. The Polish media pretended that the whole event did not exist. It was confrontation politics with a vengeance. The point at issue was: who really rules Poland? There is some evidence that Cardinal Wojtyla would have preferred a more conciliatory approach, for it seemed rather tactless and provoking to be constantly reminding the party bosses that they did not rule by consent and were kept in power thanks only to the 'friendly neighbour', the Soviet Union. But if he had his doubts he suppressed them according to the sacrosanct principle of 'the unity of the Polish episcopate': this was the entire basis of their policy. It was obvious that the government would try in various ways to 'divide and conquer'; it was equally obvious that so crude a tactic must be resisted.

But Archbishop Wojtyla had, near at home, a constant, tugging reminder that the Church could not expect to win concessions without a display of strength. Just four miles from Krakow, a mere twenty-minute tram-ride away, lies the grim steel town of Nowa Huta. It was planted there in the Stalinist period, against all economic logic, and deliberately intended to be the place where the new 'socialist man' could be forged. There are few less joyous places in the world. Nowa Huta was also intended to counter-balance the rather provincial drowsiness of beautiful Krakow, where the old people still remembered the Emperor Franz-Josef with something like affection. After many discussions, the authorities first agreed to a site for a church in Nowa Huta in 1957. Nothing actually happened except that a cross was set up as a pledge for the future. In 1960 the authorities changed their minds, declared that the site was urgently needed for a school, and sent workmen to remove the cross.

There were pitched battles in the streets of Nowa Huta. Police cars were over-turned. There were many arrests. It was remarkable that no one got killed. The authorities relented, imposed only light prison sentences on those who had been arrested, and the long process of building a church at Nowa Huta could begin.

When I first visited Nowa Huta in 1967 work on the church had just begun, and a vast crowd had gathered for Mass in the open air, unprotected from the drizzle that was falling. They knelt in the mud and spilled across the road. Lorries and buses splashed by, drowning the sound of the reedy harmonium. All one could see above the umbrellas was a chocolate-box painting of Our Lady surrounded by a triangle of fairy lights. If one could only understand – I remember thinking – why these peasants-turned-workers were here, in the rain and the mud, then one would have a clue to Polish Catholicism. The foundation-stone of the church was already in place. It came from St Peter's tomb in Rome, and bore a message from Pope Paul VI: 'Take this stone to Poland, and may it be the corner-stone on which a church will stand in Nowa Huta, dedicated to the Queen of Poland'. Wojtyla was present every year at Nowa Huta to offer a Requiem Mass for the 400 Poles murdered by the Nazis in the nearby Krzeslawice Hills. All the elements of Polish Catholicism came tumbling together in Nowa Huta: nationalism, peasant piety, mariology, defiant traditionalism, tenacity in faith.

And these values – or traits – were given added strength by the hostility of the regime. The paradox of the Polish situation was that government harassment, designed to limit the influence of the Church and confine it to the sacristy, in practice stimulated the Church and checked the process of secularization that was taking place elsewhere in Europe. This was the strength of the Wyszinski position: he positively relished conflict as a stimulus to faith. Up there on the barricades, one could make a plea for shoulder-to-shoulder unity, and no one must break ranks.

Pope Paul VI made Archbishop Wojtyla a cardinal on

26 June 1967. Though Archbishops of Krakow had traditionally been cardinals – one of them, Jan Puzyna, had
reputedly conveyed the veto of the Austrian Emperor against
Rampolla in the conclave of 1902 – a political interpretation
was immediately given to the event. The Vatican, it was
said, was trying to 'balance' the intransigent Wyszinski with
the suppler, more conciliatory Wojtyla. He had been appointed after the first extended visit of Archbishop Agostino
Casaroli to Poland and, it was rather hastily deduced, his
nomination was part of the Vatican's *Ostpolitik* and therefore
an attempt to come to terms with regimes which by now
had a look of some permanency.

What is probable is that the appointment was straight-
forwardly made by the Vatican, but that the Polish government hoped to exploit the differences between the two men,
and that this hope proved vain: it was shattered on the
rock-like unity of the Polish bishops. Nevertheless, they do
have a different outlook. While Wyszinski remains suspicious
of intellectuals and denounces them from time to time,
Wojtyla stays in touch and likes to read the latest books.
One incident illustrates the difference. In 1969 Jerzy Turowicz published a mild enough article in *Tygodnik Powszechny*
under the title 'Crisis in the Church?' It was not in the
least concerned with Poland, and merely reported developments in Holland, France and the U.S.A. It ended on a
positive note with the suggestion that, after all, the so-called
crisis was in fact a 'crisis of growth'. This talk of crisis
mightily displeased Cardinal Wyszinski, and in a sermon
he thundered against those who had dared to suggest that
there could possibly be a crisis in the Church. 'The only
crisis,' he declared, 'was the one existing in the minds of
certain Catholic intellectuals'. Turowicz survived this attack
thanks to the patronage of Wojtyla, whom he could observe
from his office in Wiślna 12 across the archiepiscopal garden.

There were other points of contrast between the two
Polish cardinals. Wojtyla is twenty years younger and welcomed Vatican Council II as the fulfilment of many of his
hopes for the Church. Wyszinski remained suspicious, op-

posed the introduction of the vernacular, maintained that a knowledge of medieval Latin was part of the Polish tradition, did not like the rite of concelebration, and refused to allow a hand-shake at the 'kiss of peace' on the grounds that it would 'turn the church into a drawing-room'. The members of the congregation were supposed to bow gravely towards each other. Wojtyla had none of these inhibitions about the Council and wrote a book, *The Foundation of Renewal*, to make the Council known and to apply it to the Polish situation. Again, Wyszinski had constantly declared that 'Poland needs a Polish theology for the Polish situation', which sounds innocent enough but was in fact a way of warding off French and Dutch influences esteemed dangerous. His argument was that 'progressive' theology had emptied the churches of the West, while Polish churches remained full. Wojtyla had never been in a theological ghetto and has kept up with his reading of modern theology. And though he shares the Polish reverence for Our Lady, he is too much of a theologian to reduce theology to mariology. Moreover, in his analysis of the Polish situation, he is less convinced that the simple 'folk-religion', stimulated by government opposition, can last for ever, and therefore more concerned to develop an educated laity as the only way informed faith can survive in the late twentieth century.

I was in Poland again in May 1972 shortly after Wyszinski and Wojtyla had both issued characteristic pastoral letters. Both were read on the same Sunday, 9 April. Wyszinski in Warsaw was in top form: he denounced a 'sacriligious crime' which was, he said, without parallel in the history of the diocese. He called for services of expiation. What had happened was that the inhabitants of Zboza Wielke, a village about 50 kilometres from Warsaw, needed a church and decided to build one for themselves. It was a crude affair, hardly more than a tent propped up with planks. They had neither asked nor received permission to build their 'church'. On 22 March 1972, 150 policemen arrived on the scene, dismantled the chapel amid protests from the villagers, carted off the Blessed Sacrament in a lorry and then dumped it in a church in a neighbouring village. It was this squalid and rather petty incident that provoked Wyszinski's indignation. After earnest discussions in the central committee of the Polish Communist Party, the government backed down, agreed that a church might be built in Zboza Wielke, provided that the parish priest was removed. Wyszinski unsympathetically replied that the government had used 'Fascist methods' and that if such an attitude persisted, there would be a repetition of 1970, when the revolt of the Gdansk workers had toppled Mr Gomulka. Every sensitive spot was touched, scratched open, and then a dash of salt was added.

Meanwhile, down in Krakow, Wojtyla devoted his Sunday morning pastoral letter to quite different topics. Though he began with a flourish of trumpets ('Christians in the second half of the twentieth century are convinced that victory will be theirs'), the rest of the letter revealed a sense of the complexity of issues of which Wyszinski seemed incapable. He discussed the different interpretations of the conflict between King Bodeslaw the Bold (reigned 1058–1079) and Bishop Stanislaw, one of his predecessors in the see of Krakow. Church historians had always maintained that Stanislaw was a holy man who had courageously denounced the moral turpitude of the king, and suffered for it as Thomas à Becket did; but from the nineteenth century onwards secular-minded historians had presented Stanislaw as a meddlesome prelate who got no more than he deserved. Wojtyla used this incident to illustrate the ambiguities of history. It may seem an odd way to spend a Sunday morning, but it was not just a history lesson: Wojtyla left his hearers to decide whether there was an application to contemporary Poland, where things are not always what they seem and the miasma of ambiguity hovers over everything. Wyszinski is impatient with ambiguity. Two Polish cardinals, two styles.

The Wojtyla style was clearly seen in the way he ran his diocese. Anyone could see him, any morning, without appointment. They were received on a 'first come, first served' basis, and the self-important monsignor would have to wait while some old woman prattled on about her ailments. It was rather like a doctor's surgery. The diocesan curia thought it was rather inefficient. They also disapproved of Wojtyla's habit of holding two-day seminars in the palace once a month for workers, actors, intellectuals, students, priests, nuns – the categories are suggestive rather than exhaustive. But Wojtyla persisted and was a particular friend of the students. He liked to go skiing and canoeing with them in the holidays. They responded by calling him 'Uncle' (*wujek*, a diminutive form of *wuj*). When on 7 May 1977 Stanislaw Pyjas, a philology student of Krakow University, was found dead in a house where he had neither friends nor relatives, Wojtyla began openly to support the Committee for the Defence of the Workers (KOR) of which Pyjas had been a member. There was a significant shift in 1977. The Church began to appear not merely as an institution committed to defending its own rights, but as the only organized body capable of defending human rights generally. The 'flying universities' also began to develop in 1977. Groups of people would gather in private apartments to listen to talks on history and economics. The Church, increasingly, provided the context in which truth could be spoken.

There were also, despite the pressures, moments of humour. When Wojtyla went for his annual skiing holiday to Zakopane he naturally enough dressed for the part. One day as he was nimbly descending the slopes at Wasprowy Wierch, a policeman watched his descent and wondered who this rather portly and elderly gentleman, who could ski so well, might be. As Wojtyla came to an elegant halt, the policeman asked to see his papers. Wojtyla produced his identity card. 'You crook,' said the astonished policeman, 'do you realize where these papers come from? When did you steal them? You are going to pay for this. A spell in prison will make you come to your senses.' Wojtyla insisted that he was indeed himself. 'Nonsense,' said the policeman, 'that's what they all say. Nobody could possibly believe that a cardinal would go skiing.' There was another case of mistaken identity in the priests' holiday hostel in Zakopane. An elderly priest from another diocese was staying in the room next to Wojtyla and asked the younger man to fetch him cups of tea, take his letters to the post, and generally show respect for his venerable years. Wojtyla did all the chores without giving the game away. When the priest discovered who he really was, Wojtyla saved him from embarrassment by turning the whole affair into a joke. Both these anecdotes also show that in Poland, where the Church has no access to the mass media, a cardinal can remain unknown outside his own diocese. That may have its advantages.

Refreshed by Zakopane, Wojtyla went ahead with the implementation of the Council in the diocese of Krakow. He gave particular emphasis to priestly education. The city has three seminaries, for Silesia, Czestochowa and Krakow itself: this is a relic of the days when a distinguished Faculty of Theology still existed in the Jagiellonian University. Wojtyla organized them into an independent Pontifical Faculty of Theology which is in the odd position of not being recognized by the state, and not being interfered with either. Its name may never be mentioned in the Polish Catholic press. He stimulated the lay apostolate in Krakow by setting up in 1972 a Pastoral Synod for the diocese. Since large gatherings are not allowed, Wojtyla turned this to advantage by forming over 500 groups of fifteen to twenty people who meet to pray together and discuss the draft texts. There was also an ecumenical dimension to his work. It is difficult for a Polish bishop to be ecumenical, since partners in dialogue are not easily come by. The 500,000 Orthodox live in separated enclaves and do not have much contact with the mass of Catholics. The 200,000 assorted Protestants, mostly Methodists and Baptists, do not want to risk being overwhelmed by the Catholic majority. Even so, Wojtyla has regularly presided over the Octave of Prayer for Christian Unity, celebrated in the Dominican church in Krakow, and on the final evening there has been an agape or 'love-feast' in the medieval refectory of the Dominicans. And among the many visitors to Krakow must be included Roger Schutz, Prior of Taizé, who was present at Mass in Wojtyla's private chapel.

But Wojtyla was not confined to Poland in his years as Archbishop of Krakow. As government restrictions eased a little, he began to travel. He was present at the Australian Eucharistic Congress in 1970 and on his way back stopped in New Guinea, where he was delightfully photographed among feathered warriors. He went twice to the U.S.A. and Canada, and attended the Bicentennial Eucharistic Congress in Philadelphia in 1976, also lecturing at Harvard. Though he was mostly concerned with the Polish emigration on these visits, he also met the local bishops and so became still more widely known.

But his international stature in the life of the Church was really assured by his attendance at all the Synods which have taken place between 1967 and 1977. He thus has first-hand experience of collegiality in practice. At the 'extra-ordinary' Synod of 1969 ('extraordinary' because it was specially convened to deal with the aftermath of *Humanae Vitae*) he was president of the commission set up to produce the final declaration. In 1971 he was elected to the per-manent Council of the Synod. The voting figures are of some interest since they give an idea of the international respect in which he was already held. And if the election to the Council of the Synod was, as many maintained, a dress rehearsal for the future conclave, then Wojtyla was not doing too badly:

1971 Synod: Election of Members of Council

	Country of origin	Ballots		Posi-tion
		1	2	
Höffner	Germany	77	122	1
Zoungrana	Upper Volta	76	—	
Krol	U.S.A.	75	91	8
Cordeiro	Pakistan	74	117	2

	Country of origin	Ballots 1	Ballots 2	Position
Malula	Zaïre	72	93	6
Thiandoum	Senegal	71	114	3
Duval	Algeria	66	100	5
Enrique y Tarancon	Spain	65	102	4
Dearden	U.S.A.	55	—	
Wojtyla	Poland	54	90	9
Lorscheider	Brazil	51	85	10
Fernandes	India	49	78	11
Marty	France	43	—	
De Araujo	Brazil	42	—	
McGrath	Panama	41	61	12
Cahill	Australia	41	92	7
Conway	Ireland	40	—	

Source: *Réorientation de l'Eglise*, René Laurentin, Seuil, Paris, 1972, p. 202.

At the next Synod in 1974 Wojtyla presented a position paper as an introduction to the debate on the theological implications of evangelization. It was widely praised. Dr Thomas Holland, Bishop of Salford, found it 'a towering, massive piece of theological reflection, carrying certain issues further than I have ever seen them taken', and added that it was 'a major theological event of the last decade'. However, under questioning, Bishop Holland could not call to mind any of its particular insights. In answer to another question about the precise authorship of the Wojtyla report, Bishop Holland rather gave the game away. He had met someone who had formerly been Wojtyla's professor and asked him frankly how much help he had received. 'None at all,' replied the (presumably) venerable old man, '*ipse solus*, he alone wrote it during his summer vacation.' The first two weeks of the Synod had been devoted to 'experiences' of evangelization and to reports from the front-line, and there needed to be some organic link between experience and theology. The interpretation of the experiences could not precede the account of them. It was this that led some observers to think of Cardinal Wojtyla as a theologian who worked on a deductive method rather than an inductive one.

But to some extent he redressed the balance after the Gregorian Professor Domenico Grasso had presented what was supposed to be a summary of the discussion on experiences of evangelization (his paper had in fact been written the previous May). Wojtyla then asked to speak, thanked Grasso for his work, but not too profusely, warned against splitting off 'theology' from 'experience' and provided his own extremely accurate and helpful summary of what had been said so far:

The second stage of our work (theological reflection) should be intimately connected with the first (reports on experiences) . . . Might I recall certain tendencies that have already appeared in our discussions and which have important theological consequences. These tendencies take different forms in different parts of the world.

1) The theme of '*indigenization*', that is the mutual exchange between the Gospel and the native life and culture of a given people or continent, came through strongly in the interventions from Africa.

2) The question of *non-Christian religions* has been drawn to our attention by those Synod fathers from the East, especially those from Asia.

3) The theme of *liberation*, in the theological, social and ethical meaning of the term, has been stressed by the Latin Americans.

4) The theme of *secularization*, together with its concomitant, *secularism*, in the sense of a theoretical and practical denial of God in the consumer society, has been well brought out by bishops from Western Europe and North America.

5) Finally there is the question of *systematic, programmatic* atheism, that is to say, the complete denial of any place for God either for the individual or for society . . .

This sentence was left unfinished. There was no need to identify the origin of these complaints. He concluded:

> In view of all this, we have to keep before our eyes not only the personal nature of the relationship to God which belongs to human nature itself, but also the basic right of every person and every society to embrace the faith and to confess it privately and publicly. This is what we should keep in mind as we start our discussion groups (*circuli minores*) where our thinking has to become theological.

This improvization from five points on a postcard accurately summed up the discussions on 'experiences' and provided, according to René Laurentin, 'a luminous introduction' to the second part of the Synod (*L'Evangélisation après le Quatrième Synode*, Seuil, Paris, 1975, p. 66). Perhaps more importantly it demonstrated that Wojtyla could keep a clear head in a complicated discussion, that his Polish background in no way inhibited his grasp of world-wide issues, and that he was not at all an *a priori* theologian who deduced everything from first principles, but that he was prepared to listen and to learn. These are all important attributes in a pope. The election to the Synod Secretariat was done this time on a continental basis, so that comparisons with 1971 are difficult, but Wojtyla clearly moved up in the league table. In the second ballot on 22 October 1974 the votes were as follows:

Lorscheider	148
Etchegaray	140
Zoa	126
Wojtyla	115
Pironio	108
Thiandoum	98
Kim	86
De Souza	84
Cordeiro	79

What was noteworthy about this election was that there were only two Europeans in the first ten: Etchegaray of Marseilles (who is still not yet a cardinal) and Wojtyla. One may also conclude that Wojtyla knows how the Synod works, and that when he committed himself, on the day after his election as pope, to developing 'collegiality' still further, he had the Synod in mind.

There was one more event in the diocese of Krakow that must be recorded. On 15 May 1977 the Church at Nowa Huta was at last consecrated by Cardinal Wojtyla. I still have the invitation, rather crudely typed and in quaint but moving English, to the opening ceremony. It explains: 'Some churches are built for people – who never come. Some churches are built by the people – to serve their pride. This is not how we see our effort. This is a house of God to accommodate his people. We build this church for our children and grandchildren and for guests coming from afar.' And now the church of Our Lady, Queen of Poland, rises like some vast looming ship in the centre of Nowa Huta. In the crypt are the remarkable *pietà* sculpted by Antoniego Rzasy: Our Lady holds her child in various attitudes of supplication and fear: each one commemorates a different concentration camp. Suddenly one sees the massive, gaunt figure of Blessed Maksymilian Kolbe, in his striped prison clothes, the Franciscan priest who gave his life in Auschwitz so that the father of a family might be saved. When people talk about a crisis of identity in the priesthood, Wojtyla returns to the example of Kolbe. The church at Nowa Huta is also a symbol of Polish-German reconciliation, for the German Christian movement called *Sühnezeichen* ('Sign of Reconciliation') contributed to its building. The intention is that the church at Nowa Huta should become a centre for the crippled and the dying, along the lines of St Christopher's Hospice in London, where the dying are helped to die with dignity. Cardinal Wojtyla, in his sermon on 15 May 1977, missed none of these points. A church is not merely a building, he said. It is made up of living stones: 'This was built as a city without God. But the will of God and the people who work here has prevailed. Let this be a lesson.' In the end the Polish experience of Wojtyla helped him to grasp not merely something about a never-say-die traditionalism but something more important about what matters and what does not in Christian faith. He was driven back to the essentials, to the survival kit of faith that is needed for the Church on its pilgrim journey. The building of the Nowa Huta church was a summary in concrete of his pastoral ministry in Krakow.

1977 was a year of great tension in Poland. It looked as though the country was becoming ungovernable. In May a group of hunger strikers took possession of St Martin's church in Warsaw. They were protesting against the imprisonment of the Radom workers, who had been accused of sabotage simply for objecting to higher food prices. The hunger strikers were not all Catholics. They included wives and relatives of the imprisoned workers, a Catholic priest, the father of a revisionist Marxist historian, a sociologist and the editors of two Catholic magazines, *Wiez* and *Znak*. By a quirk of Polish law, they could not be arrested in a church: the right of sanctuary is still respected. They were arrested as they emerged.

The real significance of this episode was that it represented a coming together of all the forces that could threaten Mr Gierek's regime. He responded by quietly releasing the Radom workers and the hunger strikers, arranging his first-ever official conversation with Cardinal Wyszinski on 29 October 1977, and setting off for Rome to meet Pope Paul VI in his private library on 28 November. Gierek went cap in hand. He is in the business of managing Poles. His local situation was becoming desperate. The alliance of workers, intellectuals, dissident Marxists and churchmen was creating an explosive situation. Pope Paul said in his speech that 'the Church did not ask for privileges, merely for the right to carry out its specific mission in freedom'. In his olive-branch reply, Gierek claimed that 'no conflict between Church and state' existed in Poland. Television pictures and newspaper reports confirmed the impression that all was well. Gierek needed the visit to the Vatican to give himself respectability and defuse the opposition. The next time the Vatican was seen on Polish television was on 22 October 1978 when Pope John Paul II celebrated his inaugural Mass and embraced, at great length and with tears, Cardinal Wyszinski.

14

Pope John Paul II

*To the see of Peter in Rome there succeeds today a Bishop
who is not a Roman. A Bishop who is a son of Poland.
But from this moment he too becomes a Roman.*
Pope John Paul II at his inauguration
Mass, 22 October 1978

When a man becomes pope, a process of mythologization
starts which it is difficult to resist. His previous life is edited
to show that he was long destined for the office he would
eventually occupy. He becomes over-night a world figure,
a partner in dialogue with statesmen and politicians and
with Church leaders of all kinds. It took some time to get
over the shock of the election of Pope John Paul II. Almost
the only thing anyone knew about him was that he was a
Pole – from which a stream of inaccurate deductions
followed: he was said to be dangerously pro-communist or,
alternatively, vigorously anti-communist. Gerald Priestland
of the BBC, who had compared Cardinal Luciani to 'a
rather tousled schoolmaster who has just been elected mayor
of his village', now compared Cardinal Wojtyla to Mr
Khrushchev. That seemed altogether too flattering to
Khrushchev. The people consulted by Vatican Radio in St
Peter's Square did their best to cope with their surprise.
'He's not a Pole any longer,' said one sage, 'he's a Roman
now.' Another said: 'Why not a Pole? After all, they are
good Catholics – much better than we Italians are.' Those
who knew him well were overjoyed. Derek Worlock, Archbishop of Liverpool, praised his powerful mind but added:
'He is certainly no mere academic. He has a particularly
warm heart, and in relaxation can be a most joyful com-

panion, leaning back at the end of the day to sing his Polish folksongs with a nostalgia matched by vigour' ('A Profile of the Pope', *The Tablet*, 22 October 1978, p. 1036).

The remarkable thing was that although Pope John Paul II began his pontificate with a rhythm of work that equalled or even surpassed that of his immediate predecessor, he never gave the impression of being rushed. He took his time. He would wait when applause interrupted him – as it frequently did – raise an admonishing hand, and repeat the phrase he had just started. He took almost an hour to greet the cardinals at the beginning of the inauguration Mass, and made a point of helping the older men to their feet. Some forgot to kiss his ring. He did not help them by keeping his right hand tucked away. He preferred instead to crush them in a great double-armed bear-hug. As he received the cardinals, with affection and courtesy, they might, as Peter Nicholls wrote, 'with no great stretch of the imagination, have been transformed into knights awaiting a kiss from King Arthur before setting off on another legendary venture' (*The Times*, 24 October 1978). To transform these balding, worthy, sometimes paunchy men into the knights of Camelot was no mean feat.

The physical appearance of the new pope and his readiness to depart from precedent were the most striking first impressions. He looks massive but not insensitive. His walk is heavy, and he seems to stoop because he hunches his broad shoulders. He has already caused Mgr Virgilio Noé, papal master of ceremonies, fits of embarrassed anxiety. After the ordination Mass he strode vigorously down to where the Poles were assembled, with Noé tugging uselessly at his sleeve, and greeted the cripples in their wheel-chairs. It was enough, said *The Tablet*'s Rome correspondent, an acute and anonymous fellow, 'to give healthy nightmares to protocol slaves until they either fade away or adjust themselves'. The same brisk disregard for 'the done thing' had pervaded his meeting with the press the day before. John Paul I had delighted and entertained us: but it was not a press conference. John Paul II, after his set piece, moved down the Hall of Benedictions in walkabout style and spoke to individual groups among the two thousand journalists gathered there. (Were there really two thousand journalists accredited to the Vatican? Or were half of them impostors?) Will you do this? Will you go there? The questions were fielded with wit and skill. He would do what he could, 'provided *they* will let me', was the gist of his replies. Those who had expected a non-Italian pope to be timorous and manipulable were dumbfounded. Asked how he felt after five days in the Vatican, he replied that life there was 'tolerable'.

But all this, though revealing of the man, was based on superficial impressions. There were already more substantial achievements to note. The most important was the discourse on the morning after his election which brought the conclave to a close. Pope John Paul I had started this strenuous 'innovation' and his speech was analysed at length in chapter 9. But the suggestion had been made – notably in the notorious interview given by Cardinal Siri to *Gazzetta del Populo* on 14 October – that this speech, which he described as 'insignificant', was really the work of the Secretariat of State and was masterminded by Cardinal Benelli. Though one cannot check this story, it did, with hindsight, seem rather improbable that someone who had just been elected pope would be capable of such a sustained and carefully balanced literary exercise throughout the night, and yet still appear fresh on the balcony the following noon. The discourse of Pope John Paul II did not give rise to such *arrière-pensées*. It was his own work. It reflected ideas that had long been familiar to him, and that he had expressed in books and countless articles and sermons. That he was helped to put it into Latin by a small group of cardinals was no doubt true, but it was his characteristic voice that came through as he leaned forwards, his head on one side, on the morning of 17 October.

The discourse grows in importance the more one compares it with that of his predecessor. Pope John Paul I presented a programme in which there was something for everyone:

his successor left the future open. The Church is on a pilgrim journey:

> What is the fate the Lord has in store for his Church in the next years? And what path will humanity take, as it draws near to the year 2000? These are difficult questions, to which we can only reply: God knows (cf. 2 Corinthians 12: 2–3).

A certain agnosticism and a sense of the *via negativa*, which are the other side of the virtue of hope, are welcome in a pope.

But Pope John Paul committed himself, without the hedging restrictions of his predecessor, to Vatican Council II. Nowhere did Pope John Paul II mention the 'erroneous interpretations' of the Council, nor the dangers to which a distinction between the 'letter' and the 'spirit' might lead. He was wholly positive:

> We consider our primary duty to be that of promoting, with prudent but encouraging action, the most exact fulfilment of the norms and directives of the Council. Above all we favour the development of conciliar attitudes. First one must be in harmony with the Council. One must put into effect what was stated in its documents; and what was 'implicit' should be made explicit in the light of the experiments that followed and in the light of new, emerging circumstances.

This blew vast, gaping holes through the defences of, say, a Cardinal Felici, who believed that the conciliar teaching needed to be brought back within the safe ambit of canon law. As for talk of 'experiments', the time for that is over, still according to Felici, and the central authority of the Church should be restored to its former prestige and domination.

But it was against precisely such an attitude that Pope John Paul II, so recently elected, reacted vigorously and

firmly. Nor were the implications of the Council left vaguely
hanging in the air. The first implication, he said, was that
collegiality should be taken seriously:

> Collegiality undoubtedly means that there will be appro-
> priate development of those bodies, sometimes newly-
> formed, sometimes brought up to date, which can secure
> a better union of heart, of will, of activity in building
> up the Body of Christ which is the Church. In this regard
> we make special mention of the Synod of Bishops.

Compared with the almost grudging aside of Pope John Paul
I, this was collegial dynamite. And there was no doubt that
it was heartfelt. Wojtyla's experience of the Church had
been, not that of an administrator who sees everything from
the centre, but that of the bishop of a diocese who had
participated, through the Council and the Synods, in the
government of the Church. He invented, too, in these early
days, a striking symbol of collegiality. At the end of his brief
speech to the cardinals on Wednesday 18 October, instead
of giving them the traditional papal blessing, he asked them
all to bless each other and to bless him.

The second major implication of the Council was ecumenism. On this point Pope John Paul II was not content
to lament the fact of Christian divisions – the alas-alack view
of ecumenism which postpones unity *sine die* – but stated
clearly the goal of the ecumenical movement as 'full
communion':

> It does not seem possible that there should still remain
> the drama of division among Christians – a cause of con-
> fusion, perhaps even of scandal. We intend, therefore, to
> proceed along the way already begun, by favouring those
> steps which serve to remove obstacles. Hopefully, then,
> thanks to a common effort, we might arrive finally at full
> communion.

I read through this passage with two members of the

Secretariat for Christian Unity. Made sensitive by many tough battles, they were able to point out nuances that the inexperienced reader might not have noticed. Thus, for example, to say that he intended 'to proceed along the way already begun' was a commendation of what had already been achieved in the various agreed statements. 'That is a phrase', said one of my informants, 'that would have been immediately struck out by Archbishop Jérome Hamer O.P., Secretary of the Congregation for the Doctrine of Faith, because he does not believe that ecumenism is on the right path.' All agreed that this first speech, so decisive for the future, was a masterly performance. If the conflict within the conclave had been about whether Vatican Council II should be curbed or continued, then the victory for continuation had been most decisively won, whatever the electors may have had in mind. The proof was that Cardinal Siri, by now thoroughly disgruntled, when asked what he thought about the speech, curtly replied that he had not listened to it. Presumably he stomped off to Genoa feeling the need to gather his thoughts and set about saving the Church from the consequences of its conciliar folly in some new way.

One thought that by now one had got used to novelties. But that same afternoon Pope John Paul II emerged from the Vatican to visit the Gemelli Hospital where Bishop André-Marie Deskur, the Polish head of the Commission for Social Communications, lay unconscious. (He has since recovered.) Pope John Paul travelled in an open car and was cheered along the streets of Rome. He was clearly not going to be a 'prisoner of the Vatican'. Pope John Paul I's efforts to break with protocol had been frustrated. His successor proved from the start that he was his own man, and would not be pushed around by his entourage. The Curia was kept in suspense, not to say on tenterhooks. Whereas Pope John Paul I had re-confirmed everyone within a week, thus denying himself the chance to renew the personnel, his successor said that he needed time to think over the organization of the Curia. He made his appointments piece-meal. The first to be confirmed, provisionally at least, was Cardinal Jean Villot as Secretary of State. The almost universal argument that a non-Italian pope would need an Italian Secretary of State to guide him through the tortuous maze of Italian politics was thus rejected. One could conclude that the 'Italian factor', which has so long, in varying degrees, distorted the Vatican perception of the world, would now be of less importance. Villot's conception of his role had always been 'pastoral': his function was to co-ordinate the activities of the episcopal conferences. This was now ratified. Cardinal Benelli fell silent. Nuncios wondered what their fate would be.

They may have been partially reassured the next day, 18 October, when Pope John Paul addressed the diplomats accredited to the Holy See at 11 a.m. in the Hall of Benedictions. There were no apologies or confessions of inexperience in this speech. It was as though he had been waiting to say these things for a long time, and welcomed the opportunity to express himself. Speaking in French, he said that the Church welcomes all peoples and found 'a particular richness in the diversity and pluralism of their cultures, histories and languages'. If anyone thought he had Poland in mind, he hastened to add that 'the particular nature of the country of our origin is from now on of little importance; as a Christian, and still more as pope, we are and will be the witnesses of a universal love'. In other words, he would not speak as a Pole but as pope, a representative Christian with special responsibility. At the same time he welcomed diplomatic relations, which he defined as 'relations that are stable, reciprocal, courteous, discreet and loyal'.

Diplomatic recognition, he added – and though an obvious point, it had not been greatly stressed in the last years of Paul VI – 'does not imply the approval of this or that regime – which is none of our business – nor obviously a blessing on everything it does or approval of the way it conducts its affairs'. What the Church can bring, he said, echoing Pope John Paul I, is a contribution on two levels:

the formation of consciences, and specific help on international problems by means of 'direct intervention'. No examples were given about what form this 'direct intervention' might take, but quite clearly Vatican diplomacy is not going to be passive. All these remarks on diplomatic activity, however, were placed under the heading of the 'pastoral solicitude' of the Church which is concerned, first of all, with men's salvation, but which cannot ignore a concern for 'the good and the progress of the people of the world'.

There was an intriguing passage on human rights, which Pope John Paul II discreetly called 'needs':

> The Holy See asks nothing for itself. What it does ask for, in union with the local bishops, on behalf of Christians and other believers who live in your countries, without seeking privileges but in justice, is that they may nourish their faith, be able to worship God as they will, and, as loyal citizens, play a full part in the social life of their countries.

This was a moderate statement of what might be called 'the Polish case'. The mention of the local bishops was important, for it meant that the Vatican's diplomatic activity, and in particular its *Ostpolitik*, would not be pursued over their heads. But the remark applied just as much to military dictatorships as to communist regimes. The question to both of them was: why are you so afraid to trust the people in whose name you claim to act? The discreet hint in the speech to the diplomats became a ringing appeal in the homily at the inauguration Mass:

> Open wide the doors for Christ. To his saving power open the boundaries of states, economic and political systems, the vast fields of culture, civilization and development. Do not be afraid. Christ knows 'what is in man'. He alone knows it.

That was to move from diplomacy to prophecy.

The 'inauguration of his ministry as supreme pastor' took place on Sunday 22 October at 10 a.m. in the morning. By now it seemed almost superfluous to recall that the changes introduced by Pope John Paul I – the rejection of the tiara, the use of the pallium – seemed self-evident. Yet they were nothing of the kind. In what was admittedly a satirical article, *Paese Sera*, the communist newspaper, had purportedly asked Cardinal Felici what he would do if elected pope. He proposed to outshine Pope John Paul I in humility. He would scrap the papal coat of arms, and instead of appearing regally on the balcony, would mingle among the crowds – seated on the *sedia gestatoria*! It was at least *ben trovato*. John Paul II is built of sterner stuff. His inauguration, witnessed by millions on television, was a non-triumphalistic triumph. It was a mild autumn morning, free from the threat of rain. Red and white gladioli – the national colours of Poland – surrounded the altar. The 300,000 crowd cheered everyone they recognized, from Princess Grace of Monaco to the tiny Pertini, socialist President of Italy. While waiting for the Pope to appear a soupy voice ground on wearily about the 'prerogatives' of Peter and his successors, and the long greetings to the cardinals were monotonously accompanied by the singing of the text, 'Thou art Peter, and upon this rock I will build my Church': they were both making a different kind of statement about a different kind of pope.

This became clear when Pope John Paul II began his homily with the text: 'Thou art the Christ, the Son of the living God' (Matthew 16: 15). That meant already that he saw his role as rock-apostle as that of proclaiming the essential faith of Peter, not as staking out a claim for himself. It dramatized his subordination to the Gospel, and to the faith of the Church, for, he went on, 'the ecclesial dimension of the People of God takes its origin, in fact is born, from these words of faith'. Peter's profession of faith was repeated again, like a refrain, and applied to 'all of you who are seeking God, all of you who already have the inestimable good fortune to believe, and also you who are tormented by doubt'. There was a side-glance at the Polish delegation, headed by Henryk Jablonski, President of Poland, who was accompanied by Kazamierz Kakol. There was a hint of his reluctance to accept the office, with at the same time a declaration that he was ready to submit to what was the mission of the Lord. It came out in his reference to Henryk Sienkiewicz's most famous novel, *Quo Vadis*. Peter was leaving Rome during the persecution of Nero and met Christ on the road. '*Quo Vadis*, where are you going, Lord?' he asked. Christ answered: 'I am going to Rome to be crucified again.' Crestfallen, Peter returned to Rome to take the place of Christ. The same story had been used by Pope Paul VI, who gave it a melancholy, resigned ring. But there was nothing tremulous in Pope John Paul's recounting of it.

Even the discarded tiara found a place in his homily, but it was given a wholly spiritual interpretation and applied to the whole people of God. 'Perhaps it signified', he said cautiously, 'the fact that the triple mission of Christ as priest, prophet and king continues in the Church. But everyone in the people of God shares in this threefold mission.' This was the basis of his work among the laity in Krakow. The abandoned tiara was ingeniously made to serve the teaching of Vatican II. The 'humanism' of Pope John Paul was also apparent in his homily. Christ was not seen as an authoritarian imposition from without, but as the fulfilment of the deepest aspirations of mankind:

> The absolute and yet gentle power of the Lord corresponds to the whole depths of the human person, to his loftiest aspirations of intellect, will and heart. It does not speak the language of force, but expresses itself in charity and truth.

Then came the plea to 'open wide the doors to Christ, without fear'. It was left untranslated on Polish television.

So far Pope John Paul had been speaking in Italian. Then he went into other languages. Polish naturally came first.

These few words (I am told by Poles) were a marvel of expressiveness. Something came through even in translation:

> What shall I say to you who have come from my Krakow, from the see of St Stanislaw, of whom I was the unworthy successor for fourteen years? What shall I say? Everything that I could say would fade into insignificance compared with what my heart feels, and your hearts feel, at this moment. So let us leave aside words. Let there remain just great silence before God, the silence that becomes prayer. I ask you: be with me at Jasna Gora and everywhere.

Jasna Gora is the name of the shrine of Our Lady at Czestochowa. It means 'Bright Mountain'. Greetings were added in English, French, German, Spanish, Portuguese, Russian, Czech, Ukrainian and what some held to be Lithuanian. But it was not the virtuoso display of languages that held the Roman crowd and the millions of listeners enthralled: it was the sense of encountering for the first time a human being of great faith and great strength, who at the same time knew about doubt and fear, and yet had overcome them. The style throughout was simple, fresh-minted, direct, a perfect fusion of thought and expression. His last words at the end of this lengthy and memorable morning were: 'It is time for you to go and eat, as it is for the Pope.'

No one need suppose that Pope John Paul is sustained merely by the bread of angels. He has bacon and eggs for breakfast. He needed it on 22 October, for his day's work was still not over. That same afternoon he received the visiting ecumenical delegations, which were of the highest level yet seen at any papal Mass. Dr Donald Coggan was there to represent the Anglican Communion, and afterwards received letters accusing him of 'betraying the Reformation' by attending a 'popish Mass'. The Moderator of the Church of Scotland, Dr Brodie, was also present, and no doubt had a similar postbag. There was a strong Methodist contingent.

Pope John Paul, speaking in French, made a short speech in which he stressed – characteristically thumping the word – the 'irreversible' nature of the Church's commitment to ecumenism. He then spoke to each of the delegations in turn, in their own languages, kissed them all on both cheeks, and then invited them to join hands together, as though about to sing *Auld Lang Syne*, as a sign of their unity. 'One half expected', wrote *The Tablet*'s Rome correspondent, 'to see cracks begin to appear in the wall of the papal study.'

The rhythm did not falter even after the inauguration. The Pope's in-tray was crowded. There were countless invitations to travel. The easiest one to answer was the invitation to Krakow for the nine hundredth anniversary celebrations of the death of St Stanislaw, due on 8 May 1979. Both previous popes had been invited by Cardinal Wojtyla himself, and he could hardly not go. The Polish government, cornered, acquiesced. But he was also invited to visit trouble-torn Lebanon, and President Sadat wanted him to pray with him on Mount Sinai when the peace treaty between Egypt and Israel was signed. And naturally there was an invitation from the much-postponed Puebla assembly of CELAM, the Latin American Bishops' Conference.

Other decisions and visits were crammed into his second week. Cardinal Felici was confirmed in his post as head of the commission for the revision of canon law, and no doubt briefed that the law must not be allowed to prevail over the Gospel. Cardinal Baggio was confirmed as Prefect of the Congregation of Bishops: there was an urgent need to fill the sees left vacant since the beginning of August, notably those of Venice and Krakow. Cardinal Poma was provisionally confirmed as President of the Italian Episcopal Conference. The spotlight which had fallen on the cardinals for three months, as possible candidates or as electors, was switched off. And somehow in this second week, Pope John Paul contrived to inspect the premises at Castelgandolfo, which he intends to use not merely as his summer residence – though the students of the English College should warn him that canoeing on Lake Albano would be a perilous exercise. He also managed to confer with President Giscard d'Estaing who, like all French Presidents (even the atheists) is an honorary canon of St John Lateran.

Archbishop Bruno Heim, meanwhile, had devised no less than seven versions of a possible coat of arms for the new pope. But Pope John Paul had already decided that he would retain his Krakow coat of arms, a black cross on a blue background with the letter M for Mary in the right-hand corner. In his work on heraldry, Archbishop Heim had written that 'the practice of using initials is completely opposed to the true heraldic diction and reminds one of the commercial advertisement or trade mark'. Pope John Paul got his way, but he agreed with the disappointed herald that the cross should be of gold rather than black.

On Sunday 29 October the Pope went by helicopter to visit the shrine of Mentorella, some thirty miles from Rome, where Polish monks guard a twelfth century statue of Our Lady. It will not be a dull pontificate. One may safely say that it will be as full of surprises as the three months of August, September and October which this book records. It is no exaggeration to say that the Church lived through a decade in three months.

One conclusion, implicit from the start, has now been dramatically vindicated. The papacy is not a static institution, frozen once for all in its present form. And popes are not just a mass-produced series of figures in white who appear on distant balconies and mouth interchangeable platitudes. It matters very much who is pope. Each pope makes his own distinctive contribution. Pope John Paul II soon indicated that he was prepared to examine seriously the Petrine office itself. In his address on the day after his election he recalled the three-fold scriptural foundation of his office as successor of St Peter: he is the rock-apostle (Matthew 16: 18–19); he is commanded to 'confirm the brethren' (Luke 22: 32); and to feed the sheep and the lambs of his flock as a witness of love (John 21: 15–17). He then went on:

We are thoroughly convinced that all modern investigation into the 'Petrine ministry' must be based on these three hinges of the Gospel. What is proper and peculiar to it becomes clearer day by day. We are dealing here with individual facets of the office which are connected with the very nature of the Church to preserve its internal unity and to guarantee its spiritual mission. This has been entrusted not only to Peter but also to his legitimate successors. We are convinced also that this unique mission must be done always in love. Love is the source which nourishes and the climate in which one grows. It is the necessary answer to the question of Jesus: 'Do you love me?'

Together with his statements on collegiality and ecumenism, this suggests that the way is now open, or opening, for the first non-Italian pope for 455 years to become the spiritual leader, in freedom and love, of all Christians. Just how much room there is for him to move is examined in the appendix which follows. He is unlikely to make the mistake attributed to Lord Rosebery by Winston Churchill: 'He would not stoop; he failed to conquer.' The narrative of the year of three popes comes to an end, but the Church and the Churches move on towards an unpredictable future, guided – Christians believe – by the surprising Holy Spirit.

THEOLOGICAL APPENDIX

From Papacy to Petrine Ministry

> It is undeniable that the Constantinian conception of the
> state, Germanic feudalism, the autocracy of the ancien
> régime and the modern centralizing conception of the
> state have, each in their turn, exercised their influence on
> the concrete historical forms in which the Church's life
> has been expressed.
>
> Piet Fransen S.J. (*Intelligent Theology I*,
> Darton, Longman and Todd, 1967, p. 40)

Dr Donald Coggan, Archbishop of Canterbury, having been
hugged by Pope John Paul II, was asked how he felt. He
replied that the Pope's three outstanding attributes were
'warmth, strength and joy'. He hoped that there would be
continuing study of the three documents already published
by ARCIC (the Anglican/Roman Catholic International
Commission) and said that he regarded the pope as 'the first
among equals'. This raised further questions. If the papacy
has already been modified under the last four popes, what
further modifications are possible? Could the pope play a
role which all Christians – or at least many other Christians
– could recognize? And what would he have to do to move
in this direction? Pope Paul VI in 1967 had regretted that
his own office, the sign of unity, had become for some a
sign of division: 'The pope – as we all know – is undoubtedly
the gravest obstacle in the path of ecumenism'.

Theologians, meanwhile, were wondering whether he
might not be the greatest asset to ecumenism. The 'papacy',
on closer inspection, turned out to be a vague, portmanteau

word that carried with it all manner of irrelevant associations. As used by Catholics and others, it tended to include everything that went on in the Vatican, its Congregations, Secretariats and so on; not so very long ago it had also included the Papal States, and though no one seemed to lament their loss, the surviving tiny Vatican City State enabled the 'papacy' to be inserted into international affairs. On its long journey through history the papacy had taken the colour of each passing age and borrowed elements from now out-dated political systems. Theologians therefore began to ask whether the 'papacy' with its historical accretions ought not to be distinguished from the 'Petrine ministry' which is contained embryonically in the New Testament.

They were authorized to raise this question by the Second Vatican Council. Although it is true to say that the Council dealt with every state of life in the Church except the papacy, it nevertheless made a series of statements which ought to have modified its exercise and opened up new possibilities for the future. The difficulty was that the Council simply juxtaposed its new emphases upon a restatement of the teaching of Vatican I. Those who wished to stress that 'nothing had changed' could appeal to the clear repetition of Vatican I; those who wished to bring out that 'change was possible and desirable' could point to the different context in which the repetition was set.

The most important new emphasis was on the role of ministry in the life of the Church. The word ministry simply means service, *diakonia*. As such it has nothing to do with power and its legal expression, jurisdiction. Ministry in the Church is based on the example of Christ who came 'to serve, not to be served' and who rejected secular models ('The kings of the Gentiles exercise lordship over them; and those in authority over them are called benefactors. But not so with you; rather let the greatest among you become as the youngest, and the leader as one who serves' Luke 22: 25–26). Ministry exists in the Church, said the Council, 'so that all who are of the people of God, and therefore enjoy a true Christian dignity, can work towards a common goal freely and yet in order' (*On the Church*, 18). The Council further recognized that the deepest source of the Church's unity is 'God's love poured into our hearts through the Holy Spirit' (Romans 5: 5). It is this which impels us to come together The ministry of unity, then, is at the service of the unifying Holy Spirit. These simple principles are of vital importance. They invite us to distinguish the 'papacy', which has borrowed from secular history, from the 'Petrine ministry', which has perdured (so Catholics believe) through various contingent historical forms.

The second important insight of Vatican II was that the papacy (or what we shall now call the Petrine ministry) does not exist in isolation. The pope is not seen over against or above his brother bishops but as one of them. His special role is in no way diminished. He still has 'the solicitude of all the Churches' but he does not bear this burden alone. We saw in chapter 2 how Pope Paul took some steps towards realizing the principle of collegiality. When it really begins to operate, the college of bishops, in its unity and its diversity, becomes the symbolic expression of *catholicity*. Whereas in the era following Vatican I it was possible to reduce the idea of catholicity to a monotonous uniformity, and to glory in it, Vatican II consciously chose another and more traditional way of defining catholicity: 'The variety of local churches with one common aspiration is particularly splendid evidence of the catholicity of the undivided Church' (*On the Church*, 23). Catholicity, then, does not mean a mass-produced Roman clergy and liturgical uniformity: on the contrary, it ought to evoke *reconciled diversity*.

This leads naturally to the third emphasis of Vatican II. It pays great attention to the local church which is seen, not as a fragment of the whole Church but as embodying all the tasks of the whole Church in the place it is. It *is* the church in Haarlem or St Albans or wherever. The Church is where Christians are. It is not an abstraction hovering up in the clouds: it has a habitat and is made up of people who can be known. The local church is gathered by the preaching of the Gospel and celebrates and forges its unity in the Eucharist. To start from the local church involved a change of perspective and a new model for conceiving the unity of the Church. Instead of the image of a pyramid, with the pope at its apex and the laity way down at the base of the triangle, a more appropriate image would be that of an interlocking network of local churches which are all in communion with each other. And they are all – the test of unity – in communion with the Bishop of Rome. The answer to the question, 'Why are you a Roman Catholic?', is that I wish to be in communion with the Bishop of Rome, the sign and embodiment of the Church's unity.

We should now be able to see the Petrine ministry in a new light. Vatican II stated its function clearly enough: 'The Chair of Peter presides over the whole assembly of charity, and protects legitimate differences' (*On the Church*, 13). This language was chosen with care: the Petrine ministry does not merely tolerate differences in a grudging fashion, it is said to protect them; and if that function is taken seriously, then it would also cherish and rejoice in legitimate differences, foster and encourage them, always providing – the text continues – 'such differences do not hinder unity but rather contribute to it' (*ibid.*). The qualifying adjective 'legitimate' might seem to make the concession more apparent than real; and this was in fact a complaint frequently heard from the Eastern Churches in the post-conciliar period. With their different rites and customs, with their married clergy, with their characteristically 'Oriental' approach to theology, which stresses the Holy Spirit, they were supposed to be the living demonstration that the Church really was the home of reconciled diversity. Moreover, they were often held out to the Anglican Communion as a model of a possible future relationship. When, therefore, their traditions were ignored or trampled upon, they had good grounds for feeling aggrieved. This feeling was particularly strong among the Ukrainian Catholics. Denied any right to exist at all in their own territory of the Ukraine by a *Diktat* of the Soviet government, forced either to go underground or be converted to Orthodoxy, they were understandably put out when the Vatican objected to them ordaining married men as priests in Canada and the United States. I will not pursue their story here. The point is simply that between the vision which Vatican II made possible and what actually happened, there was a gap. But that did not stop the theologians working on the theology of a renewed Petrine ministry.

But before they could progress any further they had to deal with Vatican I. It could not be spirited away, and no honest purpose was served by pretending that it did not exist. It was most massively there, and in its constitution, *Pastor Aeternus*, it made certain statements about the Petrine office which – to say the least – required clarification. Its three principal assertions were as follows:

If anyone says that the blessed Apostle Peter was not constituted by Christ the Lord as the Prince of all the Apostles and the visible head of the whole Church militant, or that he received immediately and directly from Jesus Christ our Lord only a primacy of honour and not a primacy of true and proper jurisdiction, let him be anathema.

If anyone says that it is not according to the institution of Christ our Lord himself, that is, by divine law, that St Peter has perpetual successors in the primacy over the whole Church; or if anyone says that the Roman Pontiff is not the successor of St Peter in the same primacy, let him be anathema.

If anyone says that the Roman Pontiff has only the office of inspection or direction, but not the full and supreme power of jurisdiction over the whole Church, not only in matters that pertain to faith and morals, but also in matters that pertain to the discipline and government of the Church throughout the whole world; or if anyone says he has only a more important part and not the complete fullness of this supreme power; or if anyone says that this power is not ordinary and immediate over each and every church or over each and every shepherd and faithful member, let him be anathema (*Enchiridion Symbolorum*, ed. H. Denzinger and A. Schönmetzer, Herder, Freiburg, 23rd edition, Nos. 3055, 3058 and 3064).

Even to transcribe such dire warnings makes one tremble.

Now if one thinks that dogmatic statements by Councils of the Church have an absolute quality, as though they were somehow lifted out of time and history, then Vatican I's teaching is peremptory, final and leaves one with nothing more to discuss. It answered all the questions one might wish to ask, and answered them for all time. It left no loophole of evasiveness. Many Catholics did indeed take this view after Vatican I, and some continue to do so. Whereas Protestant fundamentalism tends to focus on the literal and eternal truth of the Bible, Catholic fundamentalism attaches itself to the letter of the Councils and will not be budged. It was precisely this attitude that prevented Archbishop Marcel Lefebvre from understanding what was happening at Vatican II. Tradition for him, instead of being the experience of the living community, had become a row of books on a shelf.

But this is not the only possible Catholic attitude to conciliar statements. It has to be conceded that scripture requires exegesis, explanation and interpretation – the science or art of hermeneutics in short; but if one concedes that, it should not be difficult to accept that conciliar statements, too, will require interpretation: they cannot be treated as though they had no history. Not only is this approach possible for Catholics, it was positively recommended by the Congregation for the Doctrine of Faith in a declaration published on 5 July 1973. Though *Mysterium Ecclesiae* was evidently directed against Hans Küng, this unimpeachable source has some useful advice on how to set about reading dogmatic statements made by Church Councils. It will come as no surprise to anyone used to handling literary texts. It makes four main points. 1) The language used in conciliar statements belongs to a particular historical period. 2) A dogmatic truth, while remaining true, may be incompletely expressed, and therefore it may require a broader context of faith for its full understanding. 3) A pronouncement addresses itself only to certain questions and not others: it is therefore limited in scope. Karl Rahner has usefully distinguished between what is 'intended' in a statement, and what is 'co-intended'. Dogmatic statements answer particular questions. 4) A statement may be couched in the changeable concepts of a given age.

We can now try to apply these principles to the interpretation of *Pastor Aeternus*. It was, first of all, a limited statement, in that it spoke only of the pope; interrupted by war, Vatican Council I was unable to go on to consider the complementary role of bishops, as had been intended. It presents, therefore, a lop-sided view of the Church. Furthermore, the text was time-conditioned in the sense that it was a typical product of the situation in which the Church found itself in the late nineteenth century. Avery Dulles has summarized the attitudes which lay behind it:

It was an era of legitimism and restorationism, when many religious thinkers were in full reaction against the excesses of the Enlightenment and the French Revolution. Liberalism was seen as the arch-enemy of the Christian spirit, and faith was extolled as an obedient submission of the mind of man to the revealing word of God. The Church was esteemed as the chief bulwark of divine truth and order against what Newman called 'the wild living intellect of man'. In some countries, such as Germany and the Austro-Hungarian Empire, efforts had recently been made to give the national hierarchies virtual autonomy from Roman authority. Many Catholics, disturbed by these efforts, and viewing the relative weakness of the Church of England under Queen Victoria, felt the necessity of a strong ecclesiastical government on the international level ... The idea of a powerful papacy appealed to those who wanted to see the Church denounce what were thought to be the chief evils of the time – liberalism, nationalism, secularism, relativism, and the like ('Papal Authority in Roman Catholicism', in *A Pope for All Christians?*, pp. 49–50. The quotation from Newman comes from his *Apologia pro vita sua*).

From this mentality there emerged, not surprisingly, a document which flatly rejected all the aspirations of the modern world. The implicit model of the Church which sustains it is of a defiant fortress-church which tells the world to go hang. The Church was seen as a 'perfect society' which did not need the state. This was to affect the attitudes of Catholics for several generations. And it shaped the outlook of popes up to Pius XII.

Vatican II was the expression of totally different attitudes. It said that the Church should share in the world's sorrows and joys and learn from it. It stressed the importance of participation in the political order – and that could not be without consequences for the Church itself. It asserted the principle of religious liberty, against the nineteenth century idea that 'error has no rights' – a position from which Pope John Paul I admitted he had to be converted. It proclaimed the presence of grace – and all grace is the grace of Christ – in all men of good will, in other religions, and self-evidently in other Christians. It was inclusive where Vatican I was exclusive. It was welcoming where Vatican I was dismissive. Instead of the fortress-image and the 'perfect society', it had a vision of the Church as the people of God on a journey through history, dusty from travel, constantly picking itself up again, but keeping the distant goal of the Kingdom ever in view. The Church was seen as 'the sign or sacrament of salvation', its tangible embodiment but without claims to monopoly. From this point of view, conversion, should it happen, would mean 'coming home', making explicit what had been implicit all along. And finally Vatican II said that the gifts of the Holy Spirit were showered upon the entire people of God, before one began to make distinctions about office in the Church. If the Vatican I concept of the papacy were to be retained in this new context, it would be an anomaly; and the Church would be a hybrid creature with the monarchical principle surmounting a structure that had become more democratic and consultative.

Moreover, the new approach to scripture made some of the assertions of Vatican I untenable as they stood (note the qualification). Reformation and Counter-Reformation theologians had been guilty of anachronism: they had read the New Testament as though expecting to discover there concepts such as primacy, jurisdiction and magisterium which were only fully developed later. Both sides in the Reformation disputes thought they had a clear idea of what 'divine institution' meant: for Catholics it meant 'directly instituted by Christ himself'; for Protestants it meant 'what is contained in scripture'. Neither side allowed for the development which had manifestly occurred throughout history. The old oppositions and controversies were made otiose as Catholics came to realize that Christ had essentially established the new people of God through his sacrifice on Calvary, and that this people, in the course of time and under the guidance of the promised Holy Spirit, would be provided with what was needed for its proper ordering; and Protestants meanwhile came to recognize the inadequacy of the 'Scripture alone' slogan, and to admit that Scripture itself was the first limb in the living tradition. (St Paul uses the formula, 'I am handing on what I have received', in his account of two crucial events – the institution of the Eucharist and the resurrection.)

Both sides further came to realize that there are two ways of looking at the origins of the Church, two types of ecclesiology. Raymond E. Brown, America's foremost Catholic scripture scholar, put it this way: there is a blue-print ecclesiology, in which everything is given from the start, and the subsequent development is merely the logical working out of the initial premises; and there is an erector-set ecclesiology (for British readers a Meccano set would be more intelligible) in which all the elements needed are given from the start, though they still have to be assembled in various patterns, according to the needs of the Church. Many inner-Church disagreements can be explained by the fact that these different ecclesiologies are in conflict with each other. The conservatives tend to work with a blue-print ecclesiology in which the Church's constitution is clearly laid down once and for all from the start. This leads to absurdities such as that perpetrated by Cardinal Benelli, who once tried to demonstrate that the Acts of the Apostles foreshadowed the Vatican diplomatic corps – after all, Titus and Timothy were sent on missions. Such ingenuity is misplaced. The other view suggests rather that the 'Petrine ministry' can be expressed in various ways. One should concentrate not so much on what it is in abstract terms and try to discover some intemporal 'essence', but rather see what it actually does and needs to do. This might be called the 'functional' approach to the Petrine ministry.

With these principles in mind, we can look again at the New Testament evidence and try to consider it without any anachronistic 'reading back'. What is presented here is a rough summary of a long debate, and the reader is referred to the review *Concilium* (March 1975) and Raymond E. Brown's book, *Biblical Reflections on Crises Facing the Church* (Darton, Longman and Todd, and Paulist Press, 1975). As far as possible, the texts will be taken in chronological order.

Peter is clearly an important figure in the primitive Christian communities. Though Paul in Galatians 2: 9 deals rather briskly and dismissively with this 'so-called pillar of the Church', it is significant that *Cephas* should already be so well known to this predominantly Gentile community that had been evangelized by Paul. By *c.* AD 50 Peter was already the best-known of the Apostles.

The gospels, however, do not present an entirely consistent picture of Peter. In Mark he is described as 'Satan', one who thinks the thoughts of men rather than those of God (cf. Mark 8: 33). Luke modifies the harshness of this presentation, and singles out Peter for a special role as the confirmer of faith (Luke 22:32), and Peter acquires this role not so much in virtue of his strength as of his frailty. It is his weakness that evokes the prayer of Jesus. As for the famous scene in Matthew 16, over which so much ink has been spilled, it is best taken as a post-resurrection narrative which acts as a parallel to certain Pauline themes. If Matthew 16 is compared with Galatians 1: 16, Paul's account of the experience of the resurrection, the similarity of language is remarkable. Both texts contain the key concepts 'reveal', 'Son', 'not flesh and blood'. A further piece of evidence that Matthew is concerned with Peter's role *after* the time of Jesus is found in his account of the story about the coin found in the fish's mouth (Matthew 17: 24–27): this reflects a question about whether Christians should pay Roman taxes – a question that could not have been asked in the lifetime of Jesus – and yet it is significant that the story should be moulded in such a way that it is Peter who gets an answer from Jesus. This is the most basic form of the magisterium: it is through Peter that an answer comes to the new problems which face the nascent Church. The texts about binding and loosing would also be relevant here.

But the most important point, according to Raymond E. Brown, is to consider not so much the details of the portrait of Peter as the *trajectory* of the image of Peter. His 'image' is not static. It grew, expanded, took on further attributes in the minds of the early Christians. More and more functions were assigned to him. When first mentioned in the gospels, Peter is a fisherman who is to become a fisher of men. But by John 21: 15–17 Jesus' conversation with Peter concerns not fish but sheep. There have been many arguments about what authority was possessed by shepherds. But many of them miss the point that the 'image' of Peter has shifted: he has ceased to be a fisher of souls and become a shepherd; and this expresses the transition from a missionary situation in which men have to be 'fished' to a 'pastoral' situation in which the Church already existed in stable and settled communities which had to be cared for. The Epistles attributed to Peter go a step further: he is called upon for the authoritative interpretation of scripture against all false teaching. Finally he is seen as the exemplary martyr.

The upshot of these considerations is this: in the New Testament we see Peter playing many roles, serving many purposes. He is fisherman, shepherd-pastor, confessor of the faith, guardian of sound doctrine and, eventually, martyr. There is an element of indeterminacy in his 'image'. It is pushed this way and then that. Peter, then, clearly cannot be fitted into any blue-print ecclesiology. All his roles may be complementary, but they are not all equally stressed at any given moment. What holds for Peter holds also for his successors. The 'trajectory' of the Petrine ministry does not point inevitably to the papacy as it had developed, say, by the time of Pope Leo the Great (440–461). There were a number of factors which enabled the Roman primacy to 'emerge': it was the only Apostolic See in the West; well-founded tradition said that both Peter and Paul had been martyred in Rome; it was the centre of a vast communications network. These considerations, though they may rule out 'divine institution' in a naïve sense, do not however imply that the development was illegitimate or that it was not assisted by the Holy Spirit. The practical conclusion is that the papacy as we know it today, or as we knew it yesterday, does not have to be taken as absolutely normative. The same process of adaptation to the real needs of the Church could take place again. Institutions survive because they learn to adapt wisely. In a world that has become one planet, 'Spaceship Earth', the Church needs the Petrine ministry as much as ever to embody and promote its unity. But is there a service which the Petrine ministry could provide for all Christians? And how would they respond?

A positive answer has already been given to these questions by a number of Christian Churches. The Joint Lutheran/Roman Catholic Study Commission was inevitably led to consider *Papal Primacy and the Universal Church* (Ed. by Paul C. Empie and T. Austin Murphy, Minneapolis, 1974). The Lutheran Churches were invited to consider 'whether they are prepared to affirm with us that papal primacy, renewed in the light of the Gospel, need not be a barrier to reconciliation'. But that was putting it negatively. The Commission went further and asked whether the Lutheran Churches could recognize 'the possibility and desirability of the papal ministry, renewed under the Gospel and committed to Christian freedom, in a larger communion that would include the Lutheran Churches'. There is no need to stress the dramatic nature of this statement. If Luther's break with Rome was the point of departure of the Reformation, and if now Lutherans could bring themselves to regard a renewed papal ministry as not only possible but desirable, then the wounds of the Reformation could finally be healed.

The Anglicans had less far to travel. Vatican II's decree *On Ecumenism* had singled out the Anglican Communion 'as occupying a special place among those communities in which some Catholic traditions and institutions continue to exist' (13). The work of the Anglican/Roman Catholic International Commission (ARCIC) culminated in its statement on *Authority in the Church* which was published on 20 January 1977. Its main assertion was this:

> The only see which makes any claim to universal primacy and which has exercised and still exercises such *episcope* is the see of Rome, the city where Peter and Paul died. It seems appropriate that in any future union a universal primacy such as has been described should be held by that see (23).

Taken with the previous agreements on Eucharist and Ministry, *Authority in the Church* paved the way to full communion between the two Churches. It conceded that difficulties remained, and listed them, but it nevertheless concluded optimistically that the Commission had reached 'a unity at the level of faith which not only justifies but requires action to bring about closer sharing between our two communions in life, work and mission' (26).

No less significant than the conclusion was the method used in *Authority in the Church*. It did not take the view that eventual unity would involve compromise or watering down. It claimed that each Church had its own characteristic approach to authority. There is the *conciliar* approach, which is found in the earliest period of Church history and which has been reflected in the Anglican preference for synodical government; and there is the *primatial* approach, embodied in the Bishop of Rome, which emerged gradually and 'in most cases in response to appeals made to him, but sometimes on his own initiative' (17). The Commission was thus armed with its two key concepts.

Its next move was to assert that conciliar and primatial authority are complementary. As Dean Henry Chadwick of Christ Church, Oxford put it: 'A council needs a primate to make it work; and a primate needs synodical and conciliar help to free him from national and theological narrowness.' In other words, an isolated pope is no more use than a beheaded council. Thus the conciliar and primatial styles of authority represent the contribution which Catholics and Anglicans can bring to each other. They provide the harmonies for the ecumenical symphony. In the past there has been a serious imbalance between the two factors. What was now proposed was a synthesis of conciliarity and primacy, a dialectical interplay, an enrichment of both Churches. Thus moving towards unity would not be a matter of compromise and common greyness. It would be a restoration on both sides of lost values. But theologians can only bring their Churches so far. The Anglican co-chairman of ARCIC, Archbishop H. R. McAdoo, quoted Karl Rahner: 'The initative is now passing from the theologians to office-holders in the Church.'

Among them is the pope. Would the new pope be sympathetic to these ecumenical ideas? Or would he regard them as irresponsible pipe-dreams? Church leaders had so often lamented the divisions of the Church which muffled the impact of the Gospel. But would they – and would the pope be capable of the voluntary renunciation of some traditional claims for the sake of realized unity? Could they, in David L. Edwards' phrase, 'stoop to conquer'? One of Pope John Paul I's first acts was to prefer the Christian title of Pastor to the pagan title of Pontiff. To attribute this preference to humility rather than to theological perception was to do him an injustice. It was a not unimportant small step. His successor, Pope John Paul II, ratified this decision and promised to go further still. Raymond E. Brown's final comment still seems justified: 'I suspect that the side which takes the first bold step will be recognizable as the most Christian' (*Biblical Reflections on Crises Facing the Church*, p. 83).

List of Books Quoted

Authority in the Church, Anglican/Roman Catholic International Commission, 1977

The Eastern Pretender, by Lucien Blit; Hutchinson, London, 1965

Le Dossier Suenens, by José de Broucker; Editions Universitaires, Paris, 1970

Biblical Reflections on Crises Facing the Church, by Raymond E. Brown; Darton, Longman and Todd, and Paulist Press, 1978

Enchiridion Symbolorum, ed. H. Denziger and A. Schönmetzer; Herder, Freiburg, 23rd edition

'The Four Quartets' in *Collected Poems 1909–62*, by T. S. Eliot; Faber and Faber, London, 1963

Papal Primacy and the Universal Church, ed. Paul C. Empie and T. Austin Murphy; Minneapolis, 1974

Intelligent Theology I, by Piet Fransen S.J.; Darton, Longman and Todd, London, 1967

Mon Petit Catéchisme: Dialogues avec un enfant, by Jean Guitton; Desclée de Brouwer, Paris, 1978

The Runaway Church, by Peter Hebblethwaite; William Collins, 1975; revised edition Fount Paperbacks, 1978

Pope John XXIII, by Paul Johnson; Hutchinson, London, 1974

L'Evangélisation après le Quatrième Synode, by René Laurentin; Seuil, Paris, 1975

Réorientation de l'Eglise, by René Laurentin; Seuil, Paris, 1972

Catechesis in Easy Stages, by Albino Luciani, 1949

Illustrissimi, by Albino Luciani; William Collins, London and Little, Brown, New York, 1978

A Pope for All Christians?, Ed. by Peter J. McCord; Paulist Press, New York, 1976, and SPCK, London, 1977

The Inner Elite, by Gary MacEoin and the Committee for the Responsible Election of the Pope; Sheed, Andrews and McMeel, Inc., Kansas City, 1978

Memoirs, by Cardinal Jószef Mindszenty; Weidenfeld and Nicolson, 1974

Venice, by James Morris; Faber and Faber, 1960

Italia, Italia, by Peter Nicholls; William Collins, Fontana, 1973

The Politics of the Vatican, by Peter Nicholls; Praeger, New York, 1968

The Five Wounds of the Church, by Antonio Rosmini

The Fourth Session, by Xavier Rynne; Farrer, Strauss and Giroux, Inc., New York, 1965; Faber and Faber, London, 1966

Letters from Vatican City, by Xavier Rynne; Farrer, Strauss and Giroux, Inc., New York; Faber and Faber, London, 1963

King Lear, by William Shakespeare

The Vatican and World Peace, ed. Francis Sweeney, S.J.; Colin Smythe, London, 1970

Annuario Pontificio

Quale Papa?, by Giancarlo Zizola; Borla, Rome, 1977

List of Periodicals and Magazines Quoted

Avvenire, Rome
Civiltà Cattolica, Rome
Commonweal, New York
Concilium
Corriere della Sera, Milan
Etudes, Paris
L'Express, Paris
Le Figaro, Paris
Gazzetta del Populo, Turin
Il Gazzettino, Venice
Il Giorno, Milan
The Guardian, London
Humanité, Paris
La Libre Belgique, Brussels
Le Monde, Paris
Messagero di San Antonio, Padua
The Month, London

National Catholic Reporter, Kansas City
Newsweek, New York
New York Times Magazine
Osservatore della Domenica
Osservatore Romano
Paese Sera, Rome
Prospettive nel Mondo
La Repubblica, Rome
Le Soir, Brussels
The Spectator, London
The Sunday Times, London
The Tablet, London
The Times, London
The Wall Street Journal, New York
Tygodnik Powszechny, Krakow

Index

Index of Names